PROCEEDINGS OF THE 7TH IRISH CONFEREN
BASED LEARNING

PROCEEDINGS OF THE 7TH IRISH CONFERENCE ON GAME-BASED LEARNING

EDITED BY PATRICK FELICIA

IRISH CONFERENCE ON GAME-BASED LEARNING

PROCEEDINGS OF THE 7TH IRISH CONFERENCE ON GAME-BASED LEARNING

EDITED BY PATRICK FELICIA

This book was first published in November 2017

iGBL Conference

Copyright the editors and authors

ISBN-10: 1978120311, ISBN-13: 978-1978120310

Table of Contents

PREFACE

Game-Based Learning is gaining a wider recognition amongst practitioners and industry, as a relevant and efficient tool to promote and support learning and change.

This book is an invitation to explore and further understand the many facets that make game-based approaches a truly interesting and effective tool to teach and train in the 21st century. It includes seven chapters with content initially presented at the 7th Irish Conference on Game-Based Learning, a conference held in Cork in June 2017, where researchers, practitioners, students and other stakeholders met and shared their interest in games and education. These chapters touch on some very important topics including science learning, serious games for health, the development of game-based solutions, gesture-based interfaces, creative teaching, or gamification to help time management.

These chapter also depict and illustrate the challenges faced by developers and educators, as well as the opportunities that game-based approaches can offer.

Each chapter is written with practicality in mind in an effort to provide the reader with both a solid theoretical approach and background, coupled to some practical guidelines and suggestions that can be applied easily.

I hope you enjoy this book and that it motivates you to tap into the many possibilities offered by games to instruct, motivate, and lead change.

Patrick Felicia, Conference Director and Editor-in-Chief.

ACKNOWLEDGEMENTS

I would like to thank the authors for their diligent work , their enthusiasm and their valuable input in the creation of this book.

Patrick Felicia.

CHAPTER I

WE KNOW MORE THAN WE CAN TELL: GAME-BASED LEARNING ANALYTICS TO MEASURE IMPLICIT LEARNING

JODI ASBELL-CLARKE AND ELIZABETH ROWE

Introduction

Game-based learning has received much warranted attention for its ability to engage a wide audience and support deep and complex learning (NRC, 2011), but perhaps the most powerful use of games in education is as novel forms of formative assessment (Gee & Shaffer, 2010; Shute & Kim, 2014). Assessments typically used in schools and educational research often rely on formalisms (text and equations) that may present barriers for certain learners, thus preventing measurement of their knowledge (Arena & Schwarz, 2013).

Digital games present novel means of assessing implicit knowledge—knowledge that may not yet be articulated by the learner. This may mitigate barriers presented by traditional assessments and thus provide an opportunity for *all* learners to demonstrate their knowledge. Educational data mining allows researchers to identify patterns of gameplay that predict implicit science learning (Rowe, Asbell-Clarke, & Baker 2015).

This paper presents a model of implicit game-based learning along with three examples of implicit science learning games developed by our team for this study. *Impulse, Quantum Spectre*, and *Ravenous* each . Each game focuses on an area of interest in STEM education and the research on each game used different methods to measure implicit science learning.

Literature Review

Implicit knowledge is considered foundational to learning (Brown, Roediger, & McDaniel, 2014; Kahneman, 2011; Lucariello, 2016; Polanyi, 1966). Implicit knowledge is demonstrable through behaviors in various everyday activities including: implicit mathematical abilities observed in studies of gamblers at the race track (Ceci & Liker, 1986); street children using early algebra skills in their vending of fruit and snacks (Nunes, Schliemann, & Carraher, 1993), and housewives calculating "best buys" at the supermarket (Lave, Murtaugh, & de la Roche, 1984). The idea of using implicit knowledge to support classroom learning is consistent with the notion of the Zone of Proximal Development (Vygotsky, 1978) and the Preparation for Future Learning (PFL) model (Schwarz, Bransford, and Sears, 2005).

The ability to measure implicit knowledge is difficult because of its being unarticulated (Collins, 2010; Reber, 1993; Underwood, 1996). Differentiating between what learners can *express* from what learners are able to *do* may provide a key lens to their implicit knowledge (Cook & Brown,

1999). In the PFL model, Schwarz et al. (2005) suggest that studying behaviors or actions may serve as a useful lens for assessing implicit knowledge. Learning assessments that focus on behaviors may remove barriers presented for many learners who struggle with formalisms presented on traditional assessments, including a broad array of diverse learners such as those with ADD, dyslexia, and Autism disorders (Haladyna & Downing, 2004).

Digital games provide a natural and engaging environment that allow behaviors and actions to inform the assessment of learning (Gee & Shaffer, 2010; Shute & Kim, 2014). Games compel players to persist in complex gameplay fostering high-level reasoning, inquiry, persistence, and creativity (Asbell-Clarke, et al., 2012; Shute, Ventura, & Ke, 2015; Steinkuehler & Duncan, 2008; Qian & Clark, 2016), as well as deep STEM learning (Clark et al., 2011; Rowe, Asbell-Clarke, Bardar, & Edwards, in preparation; Shute, Ventura, & Kim, 2013). The design of *stealth assessments* (Shute, 2011) within games has helped move researchers away from a traditional assessment design of formal pre/post tests to measure learning. Game-based learning assessments use data generated inherently through gameplay. Many game-based assessment researchers use an Evidence-Centered Game Design (ECD) model (Shute et al., 2013; Mislevy & Riconscente, 2006) where explicit learning outcomes and measures are designed and developed as part of the game design process.

In this paper, we discuss research methods for game-based learning assessment that use educational data mining to reveal implicit physics knowledge in game data. We use games designed with carefully aligned game mechanics and learning mechanics, where the play is naturally grounded in scientific phenomena. We encourage learners to play the games outside of class-time, and teachers use examples from the game in the class with discussion to connect game-based learning. We call this process *bridging* between implicit and explicit learning. Eventually, we are working towards tools where teachers can use game-based learning assessments in real-time to see when a learner is struggling or having an "aha" moment, so they can adapt the learning experience to provide the scaffolding that each learner needs to get to the next step.

Key Research Questions

This paper synthesizes studies of three free-choice science learning games designed by our team with game, learning, and assessment mechanics aligned to specific science learning outcomes (e.g. Newton's Laws of Motion; Optics; and Bird Behaviors). To study the relationship between implicit game-based learning, classroom instruction, and related science learning; each game was studied with about 400 high school learners across 25- 30 classes, which were divided into:

Control classes who partook in their normal science curriculum.

Games-Only classes where students were encouraged to play the game in or out of school, and the teacher used their normal science curriculum.

Bridge Classes where students were encouraged to play the game in or out of school, and their teacher used discussions and game examples to bridge between game-based implicit learning and classroom explicit learning.

Differences in pre/post-test performance was used as a measure of explicit learning of the science content. In addition, educational data mining models were used to analyze each student's gameplay behaviors, measuring the student's implicit knowledge about the salient phenomenon. These data were used to examine the following **research questions**:

How do students' gameplay patterns relate to their implicit and explicit learning?

What is the relationship between students' implicit game-based learning, teacher bridging activities, and students' explicit learning.

Methods

To develop measures of implicit game-based learning, researchers coded extensive samples of video observation of gameplay to identify strategies players developed that appeared consistent with underlying science understandings. Concurrently, gameplay data logs were collected including each click by each player with a timestamp and record of the state of the game. The video observations and codes served as ground-truth to distill the game log data into features that could then be mined to find patterns in gameplay data consistently used by players. Different types of data analytics were used for each game, and even within a game to detect and validate evidence of implicit learning.

Impulse

Impulse is a tablet or desktop game intended to build implicit knowledge about Newton's first and second laws of motion. Players impart a force to guide their particle to the goal without crashing into other particles (see Figure 1). All the particles obey Newton's laws of motion and the different colored particles have different mass. The text between levels of the game briefly introduces the particles as heavy or light but does not introduce any discussion of the related physics. The game was designed with the hypothesis that the game could support and measure implicit learning of Newton's first and second laws of motion:

NFL: An object will remain in constant motion (or rest) in the absence of a net external force.

NSL: The acceleration of an object caused by a net external force is depending on its mass (F=ma). In layperson's terms, this means the heavier an object, the harder it is to move.

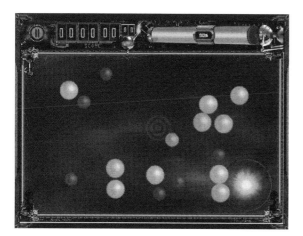

Figure 1: A screenshot from *Impulse*..

In the previous figure The player is the green particle and is going towards the cyan goal in the bottom-right corner.

To study the implicit learning of Newton's first and second law in the high-paced action game, *Impulse*, we used detectors. Detectors are decision trees, classification algorithms used to sort gameplay behaviors based on human-coded observations. The algorithms are trained on a subset of data and then cross-validated against the remainder of the data. This process is repeated multiple times to maximize reliability of the algorithms. Grounded in reliable human coding, detectors predict patterns in the gameplay data that can be used as evidence of learning. While learning theory guides the design of the game and the design of the data collection, the gameplay patterns that are identified are often emergent.

The *Impulse* detectors were built using human coding of 69 videos of diverse high school learners' gameplay. The recording of screen-capture allowed researchers to see game behaviors as well as mouse-overs (when the player is hovering or moving to a spot but not yet clicking). Simultaneously, the computer's camera captured audio and video of the player. (see Figure 2).

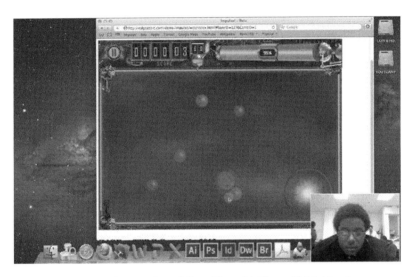

Figure 2: A Silverback Recording of GamePlay with Player ThinkAloud.

Players, often in groups, were encouraged to "Think Aloud" and talk to each other while they played. The videos were sampled and coded to identify game behaviors that were validated by player expressions and actions and consistent with player's implicit understanding of the relevant physics, Newton's first and second laws of motion. Game logs were used to build distillers and features used for the development of automated detectors. Automated detectors are binary classification algorithms that can analyze the logs of student game interactions and come to the same judgments (present versus absent) as a human being. The automated detectors for *Impulse* were applied to gameplay data from 389 students in 39 classrooms participating in a national implementation study to examine the relationship between in-game and changes in external measures of implicit understanding.

Quantum Spectre

Quantum Spectre is a puzzle-style game that uses scientifically accurate simulations of optical devices and colored laser beams to targets (see Figure 3). For each level, the player must place and rotate the lenses, flat and curved mirrors, and beam-splitters provided in the inventory to direct the laser to the matching colored target.

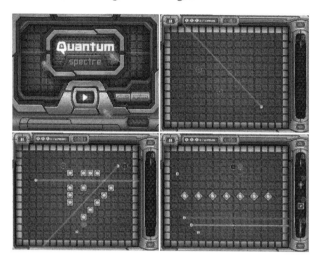

Figure 3: Quantum Spectre screenshots of 3 puzzles.

As illustrated in the previous figure, using mirrors and other optical devices from the right-side inventory, players must direct the colored laser beams to the matching targets. Source: Hamari, et al. (2015).

To examine implicit learning in *Quantum Spectre* we focus on two key science concepts:

The **Law of Reflection**, which states that the angle of incidence of a light beam reflecting off a smooth surface equals the angle of reflection. To be consistent with understanding, players must correctly rotate the optical devices to solve the puzzles.

Slope: Slope is the ratio of x and y coordinates when describing a line (rise/run). To be consistent with understanding, players must correctly place the optical devices on the puzzle grid to solve the puzzle.

To analyze data collected from the puzzle game, *Quantum Spectre*, researchers used Interaction Networks, which visualizes temporal sequences of events (Eagle et al., 2015). This method enabled great simplification of the data analysis. For example, one puzzle had 3458 unique edges (player actions) and 1800 unique game states, which were reduced to an interaction network with 22 clusters of game states that could be human coded for further analysis. Using these visualizations, researchers sorted player errors in *Quantum Spectre* in terms of puzzle errors (consistent with the player not understanding the puzzle mechanic) versus science areas (consistent with the player not understanding the salient science phenomenon).

Ravenous

Ravenous is a side-scroller game in which the player is a bird trying to fly and survive. The player controls the wing flap rate, flight angle, and decides when to land, eat, take off, and mate. For this game, although the data for data mining were collected, we did not have funds for the development and validation of data mining methods as used in the two previous games. Instead the highest game score was compared to pre/post assessment scores to see if game performance could be correlated with measures of explicit learning. The highest game score achieved by each player reflects how long their raven was able to survive, and if they were able to mate. Players with a greater implicit understanding of how birds might conserve energy during flight, how to strategically time their feeding, and avoid predators would be more likely to achieve higher scores than players that lacked those understandings. In addition to external measures of understanding about birds, researchers also examined whether higher game scores were correlated with improved interest in birds and the natural environment.

Findings and Results

In the study of *Impulse*, detectors identified patterns of player behavior that are consistent with understanding of Newton's first and second law. EDM results showed that players differentiation of mass could be detected through their game play. Figure 4 shows that players clicked more frequently (exerted more force) to move heavier particles than light particles, even when the heavier particle had a smaller diameter. This is consistent with their implicit understanding that heavier particles require more force to accelerate, which is Newton's second law. Table 1 shows that players' differentiation of mass had a significant effect on their standardized post-test scores, with players who differentiated correctly scoring higher and those who differentiated incorrectly scoring lower, when accounting for pre-test scores.

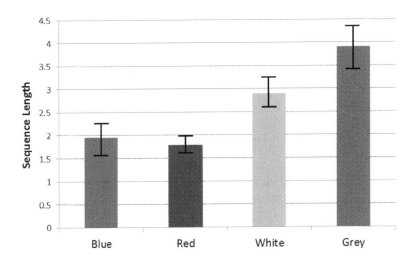

Figure 4: Mass differentiation in Impulse is shown by number of clicks for type of particle. Source, Rowe et al. 2016

Table 1: Best fitting HLM model of estimated fixed effects on standardized *Impulse* post-assessment scores with in-game measures of implicit science learning.

Parameter	Est.	Std Error	df	Sig.	95 %Confidence Interval	
					Lower	Upper
Intercept	-0.03	0.19	183	0.88	-0.40	0.34
Pre-Score (Standardized)	0.22	0.06	291	0.00	0.11	0.33
Bridge classroom (vs. Game Only)	0.39	0.14	32	0.01	0.11	0.68
Female Student (1=Yes)	-0.39	0.10	290	0.00	-0.59	-0.19
Half of students complete study (1=Yes)	1.54	0.53	286	0.00	0.50	2.58
Any Correct Differentiation of Mass	0.25	0.12	289	0.03	0.02	0.48
Any Incorrect Differentiation of Mass	-0.32	0.17	280	0.05	-0.65	0.00
Half of students complete study* Any Incorrect Differentiation (1=Yes)	-1.32	0.54	287	0.01	-2.36	-0.26

Source: Rowe et al. (2017)

In the study of *Quantum Spectre,* the percentage of players' moves that were puzzle errors did not have an effect on their standardized post-test scores, but the percentage of science errors did have a significant effect (see Table 2). Learners who made a more science errors in the game showed less improvement between their pre and post score than those who did not make as many science errors.

Table 2: Best fitting HLM model of estimated fixed effects on standardized *Quantum Spectre* post-assessment score with in-game measures of implicit science learning.

Parameter	Est.	Std Err	df	Sig.	95 %Confidence Interval	
					Lower	Upper
Intercept	0.15	0.17	13	0.42	-0.23	0.52
Pre-Assessment[1]	0.45	0.05	310	0.00	0.35	0.55
Bridge (vs. Game Only)	0.67	0.30	21	0.04	0.05	1.29
Honors/AP (1=Yes)	0.42	0.16	25	0.02	0.08	0.76
Greater than 12 days (1=Yes)	0.22	0.20	15	0.29	-0.21	0.65
%Placement Errors[1]	-0.08	0.04	297	0.07	-0.17	0.01
%Rotation Errors[1]	-0.13	0.05	307	0.01	-0.22	-0.04
Bridge*Greater than 12 Days (1=Yes)	0.80	0.33	21	0.02	0.12	1.48

[1]Standardized
Source: Rowe et al. (2017)

These findings suggest that data mining methods can be used to measure implicit learning in games. In the study of *Ravenous,* players' highest score in the game was directly related to their improvement on pre/posts tests of related science content (NKO, 2017).

In the implementation study of *Impulse* and *Quantum Spectre*, Bridge classes showed more pre/post improvement that Games-Only and Control classes for the two Physics games, *Impulse* and *Quantum Spectre*, suggesting that implicit game-based learning needs bridging to show improvement in explicit learning measures. Players in Ravenous Bridge classes showed an improvement in interest in birds and the natural game, while just playing the game in Games or Bridge classes improved related science content learning.

Discussion

In the physics games, *Impulse* and *Quantum Spectre,* data mining models were able to identify patterns of play that were consistent with implicit knowledge of the underlying physics, but bridging was required by a teacher to make that learning measurable on explicit learning assessments. This is different than studies of stealth assessments in games that often use Evidence-Centered Design and Bayesian statistics to predict learning from a prescribed set of task performances and competencies (e.g. Shute et al., 2014). While both types of studies aim to measure learning through natural gameplay, the study of implicit learning is emergent. By using EDM we allow novel strategies to emerge through the analysis of behaviors. Not only do we look for what we expect to see but we also see what we don't expect.

In the bird survival game, *Ravenous,* the score is a more direct method of implicit learning and was sufficient to predict gains on related external pre-post measures, regardless of whether or not teachers bridged gameplay and its connection to science in the real world. These differences may be due to content area, game style, or the difference (or lack of) data mining methods. The physics games may be harder content for students to learn than bird flight and behaviors, or perhaps the physics was more abstract and thus the game mechanics was not as closely tied to the learning mechanic. Finally, the bird game may have engaged students at a higher level not requiring the bridging.

Conclusion

Three different methods were able to show evidence of implicit game-based learning. In some cases, this implicit learning needs to be bridged by teachers to see evidence of explicit learning. This shows promise for implicit game-based learning assessment.

Guidelines

The process of building and validating education data mining models for game-based learning assessments requires extensive investment, but may result in a scalable method of assessing implicit knowledge from a broad audience of diverse learners. Sufficient resources and time should be allowed for adequate ground-truthing through extensive observation and human-coding.

Using data analytics as a method of implicit learning assessment shows great promise to reach learners who are not able to express their knowledge in formalisms yet may demonstrate knowledge through behaviors. The complexity of the EDM techniques, however, can make it difficult for exact replication. Results may depend on study-specific factors such as coding quality and reliability. Additional complicating factors inherent in a classroom implementation study are the comparability of samples, gameplay duration, and variability in classroom implementation.

Information from game-based learning assessments should be delivered in real-time to educators and back into the game to inform possible bridging opportunities. This has been tried by many teams using teacher dashboards but is they rarely strike the balance of easy to use and deeply informing learning (Duncan et al., 2016). Novel teaching tools are needed to engage teachers in GBL, and to support them in their already over-burdened classrooms.

Teachers will need support in bridging implicit game-based learning for explicit learning in the classroom. Bridging is an unfamiliar concept to many teachers. They may feel that gameplay is a student-centered activity that has no role for the teacher. Teachers need to see themselves as active learners and facilitators in a game-based learning classroom.

References

Arena, D. A., & Schwartz, D. L. (2013). Experience and explanation: Using videogames to prepare students for formal instruction in statistics. *Journal of Science Education and Technology*.

Asbell-Clarke, J., Edwards, T., Rowe, E., Larsen, J., Sylvan, E., & Hewitt, J. (2012). Martian Boneyards: scientific inquiry in an MMO game. *International Journal of Game-Based Learning (IJGBL)*, *2*(1), 52-76.

Brown, P. C., Roediger, H. L., & McDaniel, M. A. (2014). *Make it stick*. Harvard University Press.

Ceci, S.J. and Liker, J.K. (1986). A day at the races: A study of IQ, expertise, and cognitive complexity. *Journal of Experimental Psychology 115*(3), pp. 255-266.

Clark, D. B., Nelson, B. C., Chang, H.-Y., Martinez-Garza, M., Slack, K., & D'Angelo, C. M. (2011). Exploring Newtonian mechanics in a conceptually-integrated digital game: Comparison of learning and affective outcomes for students in Taiwan and the United States. Computers & Education, 57(3), 2178-2195.

Collins, H. (2010). *Tacit and Explicit Knowledge*. University of Chicago Press.

Cook, S. D., & Brown, J. S. (1999). Bridging epistemologies: The generative dance between organizational knowledge and organizational knowing. *Organization science, 10*(4), 381-400.

Eagle, M., Rowe, E., Hicks, A., Brown, R., Barnes, T., Asbell-Clarke, J., & Edwards, T., (2015, October). Measuring implicit science learning using networks of player-game interactions. Presented at the ACM SIGCHI Annual Symposium on Computer-Human Interaction in Play, London.

Gee, J. P., & Shaffer, D. W. (2010). Looking where the light is bad: Video games and the future of assessment. *Phi Delta Kappa International EDge*, *6*(1), 3-19.

Haladyna, T. M., & Downing, S. M. (2004). Construct-irrelevant variance in high-stakes testing. *Educational Measurement: Issues and Practice*, *23*(1), 17-27.

Hamari, J., Shernoff, D. J., Rowe, E., Coller. B., & Asbell-Clarke, J., Edwards, T. (2015). Challenging games help students learn: An empirical study on engagement, flow and immersion in game-based learning. *Computers in Human Behavior, 54*, 170-179. DOI: 10.1016/j.chb.2015.07.045

Kahneman, D. (2011). *Thinking, fast and slow*. Macmillan.

Lave, J., Murtaugh, M., & de la Roche, O. (1984). The dialectic of arithmetic in grocery shopping. In B. Rogoff & J. Lave (Eds.), Everyday Cognition: Its development in social context (pp. 76-94). Cambridge, Mass: Harvard University Press.

Mislevy, R. J., & Riconscente, M. M. (2006). Evidence-centered assessment design. Handbook of test development, 61-90

National Research Council. (2011). *Learning science through computer games and simulations.* National Academies Press.

New Knowledge Organization. (2017). *Leveling Up: Final Report.*

Nunes, T., Schliemann, A.D., & Carraher, D.W. (1993). *Mathematics in the Streets and in Schools.* Cambridge, U.K: Cambridge University Press.

Polanyi, M. (1966). The Tacit Dimension. London: Routledge. (University of Chicago Press. ISBN 978-0-226-67298-4. 2009 reprint).

Qian, M., & Clark, K. R. (2016). Game-based Learning and 21st century skills: A review of recent research. *Computers in Human Behavior, 63,* 50-58

Reber, A. S. (1993). *Implicit learning and tacit knowledge: An essay on the cognitive unconscious.* Oxford, UK: Oxford University Press.

Rowe, E., Asbell-Clarke, J., & Baker, R. S. (2015). Serious games analytics to measure implicit science learning. In C. S. Loh, Y. Sheng, & D. Ifenthaler (Eds.), Serious Game Analytics: Methodologies for Performance Measurement, Assessment, and Improvement. (pp. 343-360). Switzerland: Springer International Publishing.

Rowe, E., Asbell-Clarke, J., Bardar, E., & Edwards, T., *Bridging games and classroom science learning.* Manuscript accepted for publication in the Journal of Research on Science Teaching.

Rowe, E., Asbell-Clarke, J., Baker, R., Eagle, M., Hicks, A., Barnes, T., Brown, R., & Edwards, T., (2017). Assessing implicit science learning in digital games. *Computers in Human Behavior.* DOI: 10.1016/j.chb.2017.03.043

Schwartz, D. L., Bransford, J. D., & Sears, D. (2005). Efficiency and innovation in transfer. *Transfer of learning from a modern multidisciplinary perspective,* 1-51.

Shute, V. J. (2011). Stealth assessment in computer-based games to support learning. *Computer games and instruction, 55*(2), 503-524.

Shute, V. J., & Kim, Y. J. (2014). Formative and stealth assessment. In *Handbook of research on educational communications and technology* (pp. 311-321). Springer New York.

Shute, V. J., Ventura, M., & Ke, F. (2015). The power of play: The effects of Portal 2 and Lumosity on cognitive and noncognitive skills. *Computers & Education, 80,* 58-67.

Shute, V. J., Ventura, M., & Kim, Y. J. (2013). Assessment and learning of qualitative physics in Newton's playground. *The Journal of Educational Research, 106*(6), 423-430.

Steinkuehler, C., & Duncan, S. (2008). Scientific habits of mind in virtual worlds. *Journal of Science Education and Technology, 17*(6), 530-543.

Underwood, G., & Bright, J. E. H. (1996). Cognition with and without awareness. *Implicit Cognition.*

Vygotsky, L. S. (1978). *Mind in Society: The development of higher psychological processes.* Cambridge: Harvard University Press.

Chapter II

A Serious Mobile Game App For Adult Cystic Fibrosis Patients

Tamara Vagg, You Yuan Tan, Joseph A. Eustace, Barry J. Plant, and Sabin Tabirca

Introduction

Serious games are digital games that are created for the purpose of benefiting the player in some way. These games are considered to be interactive media mechanisms that are utilized in many sectors such as marketing, education, communication and health. For medicine and health, this could mean a positive effect on the player that could benefit knowledge, attitude, physical ability, cognitive ability, health, or mental well-being (McCallum, 2012).

In the past, researchers have investigated the use of a serious game for CF pediatrics on desktop computers using inputs to capture biofeedback data (Bingham, 2010; Bingham, 2012; Oikonomou, 2012; Oikonomou, 2014). These games have demonstrated the benefits serious games can provide to CF patients, such as increased motivation and engagement with breathing and physiotherapy exercises. Research and developed games have, so far, been limited to CF children and adolescents, however it can be hypothesised that serious games may also be of benefit to CF adults if created for a more accessible platform. The smartphone may present such a platform due to its high adoption rates (Statista, 2014) and technical capabilities. Moreover, games for smartphone are played more frequently by adults, without a restriction on demographics or gender (Connolly, 2014; Entertainment Software Association, 2017).

This paper presents an Android game that captures biofeedback data via the device microphone with a view to motivating CF adults to perform blowing exercises. The game also records data pertaining to the game performance, game calibration, and questionnaire data which is then sent, stored, and analysed in an online database. If the recorded data meets predefined alert criteria, a SMS message is sent to the user. The recorded data is then viewable by the health care team members via a web-based management tool.

Literature Review

Previous research into CF serious games has shown benefits for CF pediatrics, such as increased levels of engagement, motivation, and improved lung function. These serious games were created by Bingham *et al.* (Bingham, 2010; Bingham, 2012) and Oikonomou *et al.* (Oikonomou, 2012; Oikonomou, 2014).

Chronologically, Bingham *et al.* began exploring the use of a serious game to promote awareness of breathing techniques. The game intervention was developed for desktop computers and uses a digital sine wave representation with a coloured circle. The user must control the circles movements along the sine wave using controlled blowing biofeedback data captured through a digital spirometer (Bingham, 2010). This simple game was then tested with ten CF in-patients for five 15-minute sessions. The results of which demonstrated that the CF patients were able to control their breathing in order to control the circle, they did not experience any fatigue or exhaustion, and all participants demonstrated interest in playing the game as part of their physiotherapy. All users also demonstrated an increase of blowing fidelity in the game (Bingham, 2010).

Bingham *et al.* later developed this rudimentary game further, to include a game theme, cartoon characters, a user interface (UI), colour, sprites, and game mechanics by creating "Ludicross Racing" and "Creep Frontier" (Bingham, 2012). Ludicross Racing is a racing game that required the user to move a race car by performing forced exhalation into the digital spirometer. Similarly, Creep Frontier is an adventure exploration game which required the user to blow sludge off flaura and fauna within the afflicted game world by performing forced exhalation into the digital spirometer. Thirteen CF adolescents were recruited to evaluate the system's effect on pulmonary function. The participants were randomly assigned into either the game intervention or the control group which used the standard spirometry coaching software. The results found that the participants tended to spend more time using the game software and experienced a slight increase in pulmonary function. However, the authors conclude that a clinical study is required to determine what effect the game software had on this improvement (Bingham, 2012).

Shortly after this, Oikonomou *et al.* explored the use of a serious game to improve compliance to Positive Expiratory Pressure (PEP) for children with CF (Oikonomou, 2012). Similar to the previous work of Bingham *et al.*, the authors create a custom input for the game by inserting a sensor into a PEP device. For this intervention, three games were developed for desktop computers. "Dragon Caves", "Flower Garden", and "Pirate Quest" (Oikonomou, 2012). The first game requires the user to blow continuously to control a dragon sprite through a cave to avoid stalagmites and stalactites. The second game requires the user to blow flower seeds around a garden to achieve the required pattern. Lastly, the third game requires that the user blows a pirate ship around and ocean and coast to locate treasure and fight off enemy pirate ships. These games were tested with one CF pediatric patient and their family, the results of which found that the games were enjoyable and preferred over traditional PEP exercises, however some game mechanics caused frustration. These mechanics included the need to continuously blow for the games to animate, and the difficulty of certain games (Oikonomou, 2012).

Following on from this, Oikonomou *et al.* incorporated the feedback received into the three serious games. The authors also included a new mechanism to record game statistics, which are stored online for observation. The data that is recorded in these games include IP address, Age, Score, Number of Deaths, Session Time, Number of Breaths, Max and Average Pressure, and breath time (Oikonomou, 2014). The improved games were tested with 14 CF children between the ages of 2 and 12 over 14 days. The participants were given a usability questionnaire which is later analysed along with the collected data by the authors. The authors conclude that these games are engaging and desirable to CF children and can often perform similarly to traditional PEP techniques (Oikonomou, 2014).

One observation which can be made from the available literature is the small quantity of articles available that research digital serious games for CF. In addition to the lack of manuscripts and research available, the four papers can be divided amongst two research groups: Bingham (Bingham, 2010; Bingham, 2012) and Oikonomou (Oikonomou, 2012; Oikonomou, 2014). Furthermore, each group published two papers, the first can be described as initial findings (Bingham, 2010; Oikonomou, 2012) and the second can be described as a continuation or extensive study (Bingham, 2012; Oikonomou, 2014)

Both groups identified breathing exercises and physiotherapy as an area in which serious games can be beneficial, such as breathing technique, forced expiratory, and PEP. In all cases, there were reported benefits of using these serious games. Most notably, the engagement patients had with the games.Often, patients wanted to spend longer playing the games and stated their preference for the games over traditional exercises. Oikonomou *et al.* collected data pertaining to the game software as well as breathing data captured via the digital spirometer and used this information to evaluate the usability of the tool. However this system of collecting large quantities of data could be used for other exploratory care scenarios and analysis, such as monitoring the performance of a player over time to predict possible deteriorations in health or possible exacerbations. Moreover the data collected by Oikonomou *et al.* does not appear to be available to health care professionals and is instead viewed by the authors. Considering the exploratory nature of this data, perhaps health care professionals should become more actively involved in determining what data is recorded and analysed in the event of medical significance. In this way CF serious games are no longer used for just patient engagement, but they may also be used as an indicator of health status. Health care professionals may also use such a game data collection system to record additional care data for patients in between clinic appointments which can complement self-reported data.

Another observation taken from the literature review is that none of the manuscripts target their serious game towards CF adults and instead focus on CF pediatrics and adolescents. This may be attributed to the common idea that digital games are more effective and appealing to children and adolescents as opposed to adults. Throughout the four papers, it was expected that each CF participant would spend approximately 15 minutes playing each game. For CF adults, this regular time requirement may be restrictive to their schedules. This becomes more encumbered with the added constraint of device and machine requirements. All the serious games reviewed in the previous section deploy their intervention for a desktop computer. For CF adults a serious game would need to be developed on a platform that would allow the user to play the game in between their busy schedules with work, families, college etc. In this case a desktop computer would not be sufficient, however a smartphone may pose as a solution to this issue due to its popularity and high adoption rates. In 2012, 39% of the Irish population owned a smartphone, which has since increased to 70% of the Irish population in 2015 (Eir, 2015). Venturing outside of Ireland, it is predicted that there are 2.32 billion smartphone users worldwide as of 2017 (Statista, 2014). Furthermore, the technical capabilities of the smartphone can allow for the capturing of biofeedback data without the use of external equipment. Games for smartphone often use simple game mechanics and are designed for frequential play by using game techniques such as a score to entice the user through their own competitive nature. In a report released in 2017 by the Entertainment Software Association (ESA), it was found that the average age for an individual who plays games amongst the American population is 35 years old (Entertainment Software Association, 2017). Moreover the report outlines that games for smartphone has reached the interest of a larger population without restriction on demographics or gender (Entertainment Software Association, 2017; Connolly, 2014). As such it can be postulated that a serious game for smartphone can be of interest and benefit to CF adults.

In addition to this the smartphone platform would allow the user to play this game in between their demanding schedule, which can be regarded as more flexible and engaging than standard care.

Considering the above it can be concluded that the available research in the field of serious games for CF has been conducted by two research groups, showing the paucity of research into this area. Despite this limitation, the four manuscripts highlight the benefits serious games can have on CF patients and the increase in motivation and engagement these patients have with their breathing and physiotherapy exercises. However the developed games have so far been limited to CF children and adolescents. It can be hypothesised that CF adults may too experience benefits of a serious game for physiotherapy and breathing exercises if it is created for a more accessible platform, such as the smartphone. These benefits could range from motivation and engagement to play the game and the possibility of increased therapy compliance. Moreover, the serious game would need to be designed in such a way that it does not require specialist equipment and all inputs and interactions should be handled by the smartphone. Additionally, the game model should be designed for frequential play to allow the user to return and play the game intermittently throughout the day for convenience. Lastly the game should also record and send data to a platform that is viewable by the healthcare team for analysis. The following subsections will describe the creation of such a system.

Methodologies

Collaborative Game Design

Initially in the development of the game design, a meeting was held between computer scientists and a CF multidisciplinary team, which comprises of Dieticians, CF Physiotherapists, Respiratory Technicians, CF Nurse Specialists and CF Consultants. During this meeting all proposed aspects of the system are noted during an initial brainstorming session before being discussed more in depth. For any feature or functionality to be implemented it must be agreed upon by consensus. From this meeting, the following features were agreed upon by the multidisciplinary team, based on information used to determine if a patient could potentially suffer and exacerbation:

1. To include a Multiple-Choice Questionnaire (MCQ) to record patient baseline, and wellbeing data to be recorded daily. These questions are listed below in Table 1.
2. To calibrate the game difficulty daily, so as not to deter the user.
3. To record the patient Name, Age, Weight, Height, and Ethnicity for analysis.
4. To record the game calibration data, Average blow time, Max blow time, Game Score, and total Time Spent in the app.
5. To include a portal to allow the healthcare team members to customise the alert criteria per patient for more targeted care.
6. To include a means by which the user can control or customise game blow lengths or durations. This is to allow the user to create a game that can be modified to their own requirements, to enhance their personal gaming experience.

No.	Question	Answer Choice
1	Do you feel that your baseline is:	The same
		Better
		Worse
2	What is your current sputum volume:	The same
		Increased

3	When was your last course of antibiotics:	Decreased (calendar selection)
4	Have you done your airway clearance today:	Yes
		No
5	What is your chest physio technique:	PEP
		Acapella
		Autogenic Drainage
6	Are you on inhaled therapy:	Yes
		No
7	If so, have you taken it today:	Yes
		No
8	Would you be interested in playing again:	Yes
		No

Table 1: MCQ questions.

Serious Game Theme

It was agreed to model the game after "Flappy Bird", which was created by Dong Nguyen and released in May 2013 (Gears Studios 2013). Flappy Bird is a right to left side scroller game that requires the user to tap the screen to control sprite movement through continuously approaching obstacle pairs; a similar game mechanic to Dragon Caves (Okonomou 2012, Oikonomou 2014). In the proposed app, the user must control the movements of a sprite via biofeedback data captured by blowing into the microphone. The sprite or bird is applied with a "gravity" attribute resulting in the sprite continuously descending down the screen. When the user blows the bird jumps upwards, reversing the gravity effect for as long as the user is blowing. The gravity attribute is then reinstated once the user inhales. The bird will die if it collides with the top or bottom of the screen and with any part of the obstacles. In the case of any collision, the game is then terminated and the user is given a score screen. The score is incremented with each obstacle pair the user can successfully navigate through.

On first use of the app, the user creates a game profile which includes name, age, weight, height, and ethnicity. The user is then asked to calibrate the game difficulty by blowing for as long and as hard as possible. This calibration is done once a day. After calibration, the user is presented with the 8 part MCQ, which is also done once a day. Finally, the user is presented with the game menu which allows them to play the game or create a custom map. By creating a custom map, the user can choose the obstacle height and frequency for the game. Otherwise a random map will be generated for the user.

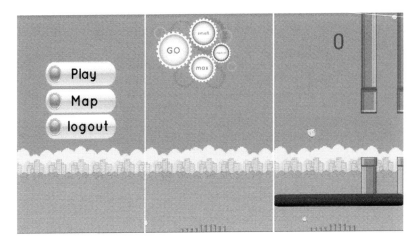

Figure 1: The game menu, map customisation screen, and game screen.

Web Based Data Analysis Tool

Once the app receives an internet connection, the aforementioned data is sent to be stored and analysed on the web management tool. A SMS alert is sent to the user if the recorded data indicates the user is exacerbating. It is agreed by the CF multidisciplinary team that the user is exacerbating if they record five consecutive increases in sputum, or five consecutive reports of worsening baseline through the questionnaire, or five consecutive poor performances in the game. If sent, the SMS advises the user to contact the healthcare team if the symptoms persist over the next 48 hours. The patient's data is analysed each time new data is entered into the online database. All the patient data is then visualised in a table and graph via a secured web tool for the CF Multidisciplinary team. The web tool also allows the healthcare team to customise both the SMS sent to the patients and individual patient alert criteria for triggering the SMS. The website can be seen in Figure 2.

Figure 2: Sample data collected via the web tool displayed via a table and graphically.

Evaluation and Discussion

The game was subjected to usability testing over two months with three CF adults; two male patients aged 26 and 32, and one female patient aged 22. Alert criteria for the three participants was not altered, and they were instead analysed using the default criteria. The users played the game frequently throughout the day (2-7 game plays taking less than a minute approx.) and regarded the game as easy to incorporate into their daily lifestyle. Patient 1 reported 100% therapy compliance via the MCQ, whereas patient 2 reported 50% and patient 3 reported 82%. Similarly patient 1 achieved the highest score (4), patient 3 acquired the second highest (2) and patient 2 received the lowest (1). This perhaps demonstrates some correlation between therapy compliance and game performance. However, this data will need to be further explored in a clinical setting before any such conclusions can be drawn.

During the two months, the users did not receive any SMS alerts, however there were on average two consecutive recordings of worsening baseline, increased sputum, or poor game performance. The users agreed that they felt an SMS alert was not required during this time, and agreed that five consecutive reports would be an accurate measure to send an alert. The participants also suggested incorporating "I don't know" or "Don't remember" as an option in the MCQ questions. During the initial testing, the users reported difficulty in blowing into the device microphone and viewing the screen. This was later resolved by using the microphone attached to headphones intended for use with smartphones. No further issues were reported once this solution was implemented. The users also commented that they enjoyed how the app does not appear to be for CF specifically, and felt comfortable playing the game with friends or in public. All users agreed they would play the game again. Over the two months, each user played the game a minimum of twice per week. Similar to the manuscripts presented in the literature review, all users regarded the game as engaging and agreed they would play it again in future. It was also found from the data collected and the comments received by the participants that the app is a usable and sufficient platform to support serious games for CF. This is again mirrored in the findings from the literature review where the data collected by the authors demonstrated that a desktop computer and USB spirometer was an usable platform for serious games for CF pediatrics. However, unlike the manuscripts described in the literature review, this serious game must be seamlessly incorporated into a CF adults daily routine including work, college, and family life. From this small pilot study, it was found that the smartphone serious game presented can achieve this task. One feature presented in this research which is unique from the manuscripts reviewed is the use of an SMS alert system. This can perhaps be attributed to the different levels of self–management requirements found between a CF pediatric and adult. Although this feature is encompassed in this research, no alerts were sent during the duration of a pilot study and further testing is required to evaluate its use.

The game was also presented to the CF Multidisciplinary team for review. During this meeting, the CF multidisciplinary team advised that physiotherapy techniques could not be translated into a game format without using an external device such as a spirometer, and as such suggested this for future developments. However, to be effectively implemented the spirometer device will need to be small and compatible with a smartphone. The team also advised that sudden blows should be recorded via the app to aid in determining the fidelity and control the users have over their breathing exercises.

Conclusion

In conclusion, a serious game smartphone app and web analysis tool for CF adults has been presented in this paper. Through ongoing patient stress testing, the system has been found to be both engaging among patients and functional. However, as the exploratory game data is still in its infancy further analysis is required with a larger cohort of CF adults. It is anticipated that this system and its framework can also be used in other medical and health areas.

Guidelines

Future games that are developed for CF adults should be developed on platforms that are easily accessible and convenient. The game intervention should also be developed so that it can be used frequently throughout the day in between the user's busy schedule. The data that is recorded via the microphone is exploratory and requires further observation and analysis to determine its use. It is suggested that this is studied more in depth before incorporating into future serious game apps. Alternatively, it is suggested that a smartphone spirometry device is incorporated. Lastly tools that incorporate an alert or analysis system must allow these criteria to be individualised for each patient, as doing so provides a more targeted approach to the intervention, with the potential of greater benefits for the patient.

Acknowledgements

We would like to acknowledge funding from the European Commission for CFMATTERS, Grant agreement 603038.

References

Bingham, P.M., Bates, J.H., Thompson-Figueroa, J. and Lahiri, T., 2010. A breath biofeedback computer game for children with cystic fibrosis. Clinical Pediatrics.

Bingham, P.M., Lahiri, T. and Ashikaga, T., 2012. Pilot trial of spirometer games for airway clearance practice in cystic fibrosis. Respiratory care, 57(8), pp.1278-1284.

Connolly, A. 2014. Who was playing games in 2014? Half a billion people.... [online] Available at: http://www.thejournal.ie/who-are-the-gamers-1780268-Dec2014/ [Accessed 9 May 2017].

Eir. 2015. eir Connected Living Survey. [online]. Available at: https://www.eir.ie/opencms/export/sites/default/.content/pdf/pressreleases/eir-_connected-_living_survey.pdf [Accessed 2 February 2017].

Entertainment Software Association, 2017. Essential Facts About the Computer and Video Game Industry. [online]. Available at: http://essentialfacts.theesa.com/mobile/ [Accessed 9 May 2017].

Gears Studios 2013, 2013. Flappy Bird. [online]. Available at: https://flappybird.me/ [Accessed 9 May 2017].

McCallum, S., 2012. Gamification and serious games for personalized health. Stud Health Technol Inform, 177(2012), pp.85-96.

Oikonomou, A. and Day, D., 2012, July. Using serious games to motivate children with cystic fibrosis to engage with mucus clearance physiotherapy. *In Complex, Intelligent and Software Intensive Systems (CISIS), 2012 Sixth International Conference* on (pp. 34-39). IEEE.

Oikonomou, A., Hartescu, D., Day, D. and Ma, M., 2014. Computer games physiotherapy for children with cystic fibrosis. In *Virtual, Augmented Reality and Serious Games for Healthcare 1* (pp. 411-443). Springer Berlin Heidelberg.

Statista, 2014. Number of smartphone users worldwide from 2014 to 2020 (in billions). [online]. Available at: https://www.statista.com/statistics/330695/number-of-smartphone-users-worldwide/ [Accessed 9 May 2017]

Chapter III

Case studies on factors influencing game selection and development by business game companies.

Kasyoka Mwanzia

Introduction

It is no doubt that business games developed for learning face the challenge of keeping up with the rapid visual and technological developments seen in entertainment games. "The difficulty of developing a serious game cannot be overstated. There are high expectations of gamers who have experienced the benefits of the multibillion dollar industry of entertainment games" (Graesser, 2017, pp.205). The move away from using entertainment games for learning has produced a considerable library of off-the-shelf serious games for fields like management and planning that address issues like strategic change and decision making. However, the decisions on which game to use is still a challenging process particularly for a manager with little to no prior knowledge on how to evaluate and subsequently chose a business game. As a result, this decision is one that is often deferred to the business game company responsible for the implementation of the game-based training. To tap into the knowledge of business game companies and create insights for organisational manager, this study asks **how do business game companies develop the appropriate solution for organisations seeking a game-based tool to address organisational challenges?** This study seeks to discover the motivations and decision making processes of business game companies as they seek to increase the reach and scope of game-based learning within organisations. By conducting interview-based case studies with business game companies, this study identifies principles such as: perceived value, focal competencies, and situational considerations. These are insights that can assist in informed development of business games as well as potentially increase their frequency of use.

Literature Review

The analysis of games for learning appears to be divided into two main schools: the study of the player and players' experience, and the study of the game itself. On the one hand, the focus of serious games scholars has been on understanding player experience with constructs such as engagement and flow, and in identifying the game features that support these constructs. Considering that individual player experience constructs are likely to be subjective, other studies have chosen to focus on the measurement of learning outcomes with knowledge and skill acquisition being the most frequently used evaluation yardstick (Boyle et al., 2016; Calderón & Ruiz, 2015). On the other hand, scholars of the game itself have focused on translating the relationship between the tools of game play (game mechanics) and the game's instructional purpose. To create these linkages, these studies have worked towards providing frameworks that itemise and then link game mechanics to learning mechanics (Amory, 2007; Arnab et al., 2015; Carvalho et al., 2015). These models however require a profound level of understanding with regards to game taxonomies and are difficult for managers with little or no game analysis knowledge to use and apply. The limitations with approaching either the player or the game is that this "focus[es]s on the learning of individuals in formal training or the educational context [with] little attention to the learning of teams, groups, organisations, networks or systems in a policy or organisational context" (Mayer, et al., 2014, pp.509).

Rather than having a business game as the sole instructional tool, organisational learning contexts consist of predominantly blended learning environments with the game as just one piece of the puzzle to a multi-pronged solution. Blended learning - where learning is orchestrated by other learning activities that bookend the game play session - stems from Kolb's (1984, pp.51) learning cycle: ways of grasping experience (concrete experience and abstract conceptualisation), and ways of transforming experiences (reflective observation and active experimentation). This is an iterative process that mixes up the actions of 'Do-Observe-Think-Plan'.

Ready-to-use off the shelf games for use in organisations are typically developed to ensure that their context of application can be flexible. This means that any one business game can be used to address one or more organisational challenges. This is achieved by using portability or bootstrapping as features of the game design (Kollars and Rosen, 2015). Portable business games are those where "the framework and the mechanics stay consistent but the subject matter, case, approach, or debriefing changes according to the needs of the particular" situation (Kollars and Rosen, 2015, pp.204). The most common example of portability in business games is seen in the use of cases. For example, a business game such as Changesetter (Relation Technologies, n.d.) - that is designed to tackle the management of change situations within organisations – has different cases to address different scenarios such as the introduction of a new system in the office or just as easily, the merger between two companies. By concentrating on the general dynamics of the issue to be addressed, the business game is repurposed with either off-the-shelf cases that closely align with the organisational challenge, or with customised cases that use the precise organisational issues all within a solid game framework.

Bootstrapping on the other hand removes this fidelity to the real-world organisational situation and calls on the users of the game to engage in abstract play. For example, a business game like Jonathon Strangeways (Elgood Effective Learning, n.d.) that uses the investigation and solving of a murder mystery to addresses organisational challenges like problem solving, team skills and communication. In abstract play, players indirectly explore themes such as their communication style through how they share clues and become aware of how individual behaviour affects teamwork. By stepping away from the real situation, players may escape situational paralysis and experience more freedom to speak out and participate without fear of doing the wrong thing, or of receiving judgement from colleagues or superiors. A point of note is that bootstrapping requires a certain level of common knowledge since players are called upon to draw "from culturally available contexts as the first foothold in the game" (Kollars and Rosen, 2015, pp.206). In addition, while it is usually the case that the use of a business game does not focus only on the game play and typically would not end in a vacuum, when using a bootstrapped game the debriefing process becomes particularly essential. Tying the learning outcomes to the experiences within the simulation, debriefing revisits the organisational challenges that inspired the use of the game play and ensures that connections are made to the users' real world situations.

Method

As the nature of the inquiry was exploratory, the choice of qualitative inquiry was warranted. This consisted of interview-based case studies of five business game companies. The cases were selected based on purposeful sampling and consisted of five business game companies of varying company size from five different countries: Canada, Denmark, England, Germany and the Netherlands. The interview participants were individuals who are knowledgeable in the selection, development and adaptation of business games. All but one of the participants held the top managerial role in the company and all five participants were active facilitators of their games. The interviews were conducted as semi structured conversational interviews with the bulk of the interview questions focused around opinion and values regarding the study topic. The interviews all lasting about an hour in duration were conducted in March and April 2017. Three of the interviews were conducted in person, one over skype and the last as a telephone interview. All interviews were voice recorded and later transcribed and coded using NVivo software. The data analysis was carried out using Creswell's (2009, pp.183-190) six step process.

Theoretically, the interview participants have been approached as cultural intermediaries who play a role as go-betweens between the sites of production of game development and the sites of use. As seen in the literature review, the bulk of research within the field of serious games has its focus on either the sites of production – the study of the game – or on the sites of use – the study of the players. Little or no attention has been paid to the cultural intermediaries who play the role of 'transmission belt' between the two sites (Bourdieu, 1984). Even though all but one of the interview participants are involved in the development of business games, this study has approached the business game companies within their roles as mediators between the game designers/developers and the organisation looking for a game-based tool.

Findings and Results

The following findings are based on themes that emerged from the interviews with the business game companies to answer the research question **how do business game companies develop the appropriate solution for organisations seeking a game-based tool to address organisational challenges**? Investigations were made into where business game companies perceive the learning happens; what concerns there were with using business games designed as a framework to be used across different business sectors; and how these concerns influenced the choice between off-the-shelf and bespoke games.

Motivations for game use

Overall, the use of games for learning in organisations was based on the concern that learning within the work environment was not only boring but also ineffective. The interview participants expressed concern that PowerPoint presentations predominate organisational learning, methods that ignore the fact that for transfer to occur between training and the real world, experiential learning is necessary. Besides being an innovative and active approach, participants indicated that the business game tool could respond to the needs of an organisation to absorb new competencies in a fairly short amount of time with a high number of people. Most participants indicated that visual motifs and symbols like seeing the actual cash flow of a company through the physical representation of tokens, or in getting your team members to get on board a boat as a symbol for agreement, played a key role in creating understanding The interview participants discussed the triggers that stimulated either the selection of an existing game or the development of a new one. The triggers fell into one or more of the following: client need; a gap in the industry or in the game companies' portfolio; or the interest in the translation of a business related theoretical framework into a game solution.

Game Type

Majority of the clients of the business game companies were using an off-the-shelf game from the business game company's portfolio. Most of the off-the-shelf games were customised to the client's challenge using a relevant game scenario also referred to as a game 'case'. Depending on the game platform, customised cases could also be created. Per year, only an estimated five to six bespoke games were developed. Besides time and the commitment on the part of the client towards the process involved in developing a bespoke game, the financial entry point was still relatively high with one participant indicating a time investment of two to four months with a financial outlay from 20,000 Euros to as much as 200,000 Euros. Four out of five of the interview participants were predominantly using board games, a couple of which are being run with a computer to aid with the calculation of the metrics within the game.

Perception of learning: An important aspect that emerged was that business games are rarely used as a stand-alone solution and are a usually a part of a broader learning process that involves bookending the game play with presentations, breakout groups, workshops, seminars. With this in mind, the interview participants observed that there are several touch points where learning happens: in game play, through reflective dialogue, and during application to the real-world situation. All the interview participants zeroed in on the aspect of transfer from the game play scenario to their real-world situation as being the one where the highest value lay.

Learning Structure

As part of the blended learning, the business game companies occasionally exposed the users to some introductory materials before the game play session. Most games are divided into rounds with breaks in between for reflection during which the facilitators will tend to focus on the reflection of the outcomes of the game play thus far. Occasionally, theoretical or research-based materials is presented during these breaks to support the metrics or the mechanics that the users had experienced during the game play. Interestingly, this supplementary information is presented to the users by use of conventional learning methods such as PowerPoint presentations or reading materials. A debriefing session allows the players to discuss the application of the game play towards their real-world contexts. Only one case out of five provided the players the chance to return to the game play to review their in-game choices and outcomes once they had returned to their work situation.

Discussion

The interview responses place critical emphasis on the concept of transfer: that connections will happen between the learning space and the real world. This situates the value of game-based learning along the axis of transforming experience of Kolb's (1984) learning cycle. This is the continuum between reflecting on the experience and testing out what was learned during the experience. This emphasis does not exclude the other stages within the experiential learning cycle, rather points out that business game companies are particularly attentive to ensure that dialogue takes place to enable shared learning within the group, and planning for transfer is addressed for complete execution of all stages of the learning cycle. Decision making is then based around the following considerations:

1. Learning Competencies: Which strategic or affective outcome is the main targeted objective? What do the players need to learn?
2. Blended Learning Situations: Besides the game play session, what other activities will be needed for complete execution of all stages of the learning cycle? How do the players need to learn?
3. Facilitation: What role does the facilitator need to play to ensure that both learning and transfer happen?
4. Portability & Bootstrapping: What level of fidelity to the real-world situation is required to effect this learning?
5. Resources: What are the considerations of time, finances, or commitment on the part of the organisation?

The study reveals that game choice is based on perceived value (where learning happens), focal competencies, and situational considerations. Similar to game studies that focus on player experience (Boyle et al., 2016), this study reveals that the focus of business game companies is on the learning experience of the player. However, the findings differ wherein rather than emphasising the learning of the individual, prominence is given to learning within the group through a shared game play experience and reflective dialogue. The study also highlights that in most cases, learning goals were linked to game scenarios rather than to game mechanics. One may surmise that the frameworks available for the itemisation and linking of game mechanics to learning goals (Amory, 2007; Arnab et al., 2015; Carvalho et al., 2015) can be useful at the game development phase, whereas during implementation, the focus is on the game play situation rather than the nuts and bolts of the game play. There is the unmistakable influence of tacit knowledge on the part of the game company that is significant though unquantifiable. This tacit knowledge includes the ability to understand the organisation's challenge in the real-world, and to translate this challenge into an identifiable gap in competencies. This comprehension also encompasses grasp of both the learning situation and the players to be able to facilitate dialogues that will lead to transfer.

Conclusion

It would be interesting for active observations of learners in their real world organisational contexts after the game-based intervention to be made. Further research structured as long term observational research within organisations to obtain demonstrable knowledge by documenting the learning transfer would provide data on the nature and effectiveness of transfer after the use of a game-based learning tool.

Building a community of reference in the form of a business game database would be beneficial in identifying developments and trends within the development of business games. The most significant cataloguing of business games is the 1997 assessment by Chris Elgood (Elgood, 1997) with 354 games (Greco et al., 2013). This is a gap that remains to be filled and would provide a rich resource for organisation, researchers as well as developers.

Guidelines

What does this mean for managers who are considering the use of organisational games?

- Keep in mind that a business game should be part of a larger management process within the organisation.
- Bookend the game with other activities that will encourage dialogue, reinforce the learning within your team and ensure transfer to the real-world challenge.
- Do not be afraid to make use of a bootstrapped game tool that is not explicitly built around the organisational scenario. With skilled and insightful facilitation, a simple game can lead to a rich learning experience.

References

Amory, A., 2006. Game object model version II: a theoretical framework for educational game development. Education Tech Research Dev 55, 51–77. doi:10.1007/s11423-006-9001-x

Arnab, S., Lim, T., Carvalho, M.B., Bellotti, F., de Freitas, S., Louchart, S., Suttie, N., Berta, R., De Gloria, A., 2015. Mapping learning and game mechanics for serious games analysis: Mapping learning and game mechanics. British Journal of Educational Technology 46, 391–411. doi:10.1111/bjet.12113

Bourdieu, P., 1984. Distinction: A Social Critique of the Judgement of Taste. Harvard University Press.

Boyle, E.A., Hainey, T., Connolly, T.M., Gray, G., Earp, J., Ott, M., Lim, T., Ninaus, M., Ribeiro, C., Pereira, J., 2016. An update to the systematic literature review of empirical evidence of the impacts and outcomes of computer games and serious games. Computers & Education 94, 178–192. doi:10.1016/j.compedu.2015.11.003

Calderón, A., Ruiz, M., 2015. A systematic literature review on serious games evaluation: An application to software project management. Computers & Education 87, 396–422. doi:10.1016/j.compedu.2015.07.011

Carvalho, M.B., Bellotti, F., Berta, R., De Gloria, A., Sedano, C.I., Hauge, J.B., Hu, J., Rauterberg, M., 2015. An activity theory-based model for serious games analysis and conceptual design. Computers & Education 87, 166–181. doi:10.1016/j.compedu.2015.03.023

Creswell, J.W., 2009. Research design: qualitative, quantitative, and mixed methods approaches, 3rd ed. ed. Sage Publications, Thousand Oaks, Calif.

Graesser, A.C., 2017. Reflections on Serious Games, in: Wouters, P., van Oostendorp, H. (Eds.), Instructional Techniques to Facilitate Learning and Motivation of Serious Games. Springer International Publishing, Cham, pp. 199–212. doi:10.1007/978-3-319-39298-1_11

Elgood Effective Learning, n.d. Jonathon Strangeways. [business game]. Available at:< https://www.chris-elgood.com/product/jonathon-strangeways/>[Accessed 10 March 2017].

Elgood, C., 1997. Handbook of Management Games and Simulations. Gower.

Greco, M., Baldissin, N., Nonino, F., 2013. An exploratory taxonomy of business games. Simulation & Gaming 44, 645–682.

Kollars, N., Rosen, A., 2015. Bootstrapping and Portability in Simulation Design. International Studies Perspectives 202–213. doi:10.1093/isp/ekv007

Kolb, D.A., 2014. Experiential Learning: Experience as the Source of Learning and Development. FT Press.

Mayer, I., Bekebrede, G., Harteveld, C., Warmelink, H., Zhou, Q., van Ruijven, T., Lo, J., Kortmann, R., Wenzler, I., 2014. The research and evaluation of serious games: Toward a comprehensive methodology: The research and evaluation of serious games. British Journal of Educational Technology 45, 502–527. doi:10.1111/bjet.12067

Relation   Technologies,   n.d.   Changesetter.   [business   game].   Available   at:< http://relationtechnologies.com/concepts/changesetter/> [Accessed 24 February 2017].

CHAPTER IV

ASSESSMENT OF GESTURE-BASED NATURAL INTERFACE SYSTEMS FOR SERIOUS GAMES

DAVID MURPHY AND KARINA DUBÉ

Introduction

Since the 1990s computer based learning and its application to various fields of medicine and surgery have become popular in medical education (Gorman, 2000; Bradley, 2006; Murphy, 2008). With respect to surgery, the emphasis in computer-based learning has been on the acquisition of skills – where students learn new procedures and skills, and practice them in a safe environment – and described by Kneebone as a "Zone of Clinical Safety" (2003). Furthermore, the area of medical and surgical training lends itself to more immersive forms of computer based learning, such as game-based learning and Virtual Reality based learning (Gallagher, 2005; McCloy, 2001; Sliney, 2011).

The goal of the current study is to examine interaction designs and devices for natural gesture-based interaction in a 3D serious game for surgical training. The surgical procedure of interest is the Laparoscopic Cholecystectomy, more commonly known as Gall Bladder Removal. While this procedure is very common, it has a relatively high error rate associated with it, hence it is the focus of a lot of training simulators. As the procedure is laparoscopic, that is minimally invasive and conducted through an endocscopic camera and instruments, it is an ideal candidate for serious game-based learning (Murphy, 2008). The current version of our surgical training system is built in Unreal Engine 4 (UE4), incorporating the PhysX engine and Flex Particle system, with a First-Person perspective. For the current phase of research, we wanted to examine the feasibility of incorporating gesture-based natural interface input methods. As part of this investigation, we compared the use of a conventional computer mouse, non-haptic data glove (5DT Data Glove), and non-contact gesture input system (Leap Motion sensor) in the selection and manipulation of a simple deformable virtual object.

The 3D model used for interaction was a particle-based deformable object using NVIDIA Flex, which is a particle based simulation system for real-time visual effects. FleX uses a unified particle representation for all object types, which facilitates new effects where different simulated substances can interact with each other seamlessly. FleX is designed to take advantage of GPUs acceleration making these effects possible in real-time applications, such as games and VR. The interface was constructed in C++ in the Unreal Engine 4 game engine. The Unreal Engine 4 is an advanced set of software tools for the development and compilation of sophisticated games and VR experiences. The interface was designed to measure the movement of the wrist around a virtual object.

Previous Work

Today we are seeing the widespread availability and commoditisation of consumer-grade virtual reality hardware, however the interaction and design concepts are not yet established and are an active area of research.

As we move toward total immersiveness, we need to adopt new modes of interacting within that immersive space. The mouse model is very effective when working with 2D interfaces and spaces, and can be mapped neatly to the physical action of moving a mouse on a table. In 3D space, the naturalness is hindered and limited by the 2D constraints of the mouse. Since the planes of motion in 3D can be dissimilar to those available in 2D, the mouse-driven techniques to compensate for this tend to be complicated, cumbersome and somewhat contrived (Herndon, 1994). To address these inherent difficulties, alternative techniques have been proposed by looking at how we interact in the real world and developing corresponding tangible interfaces with appropriate affordances. While speech can be used in some aspects of virtual interaction, dexterous tasks require more direct, manipulative interactions as associated with hand based interfaces. This can be challenging as the computer has to track and interpret the movements, positions and intentions of the user. Interactions have been classified into contact and non-contact means. Contact refers to devices using the "sensors and some kinds of hardware to construct the gesture capturing mechanism" (Weng 2015) and includes devices such as gloves, wands, and touch screens. Non-contact refers to the "vision-based technique which offers more natural interaction without using wearable devices in the hands," (Weng 2015) and include devices such as the Leap Motion and Kinect.

Gestural interfaces for interacting in 3D space, and in particular techniques for navigating and interacting in virtual space have not been tied down and are active areas of research. In 3D user interfaces several tasks are common to most systems - navigation, selection, and manipulation are three of the most common (Bowman, 2004). LaViola, as part of a course given at SIGGRAPH 2011, outlined the various means of these interactions (LaViola, 2011). For selection, defined as "the process of accessing one or more objects in a 3D virtual world", several implementation aspects need to be considered. Triggering of the selection event, feedback regarding the selected object, and efficiency in detecting selectable objects. The most common selection technique is a virtual hand, which selects based on collision with virtual objects, followed by the ray-casting technique which casts a vector (ray) in to a virtual scene and selects the object that it first intersects with. The first method is more akin to real life explorative manipulation while the second allows for more direct and greater accuracy and efficiency.

Manipulation can be seen as an extension of the selection process, and so careful integration between the two techniques is important. Additionally, the selection mode must be turned off when switched to manipulation mode and consideration of the outcome of releasing the selection must be given.

In the current study we have implemented a version of Hand-Centered Object Manipulation Extending Ray-Casting (HOMER – Lawrence, 1997). The metaphor of the laser pointer is adopted for selecting objects, as it allows the user to see what is actually being selected without "physically" touching the model in virtual space. However, once the selection is made, it switches to the "virtual hand" method for manipulating the object. The system modifies both of these methods by having the ray-casting operate on the area of a hemisphere for selection, while the virtual hand representation is simply the pull and push, indicated by the disk, with the intent of the user is inferred by the direction they move their hands. This adapted hybrid approach, especially in the context of Virtual Reality, was first recommended by Pavlovic (Pavlovic, 1997), and further explored by Mitra et. Al (Mitra, 2007).

Methods

To evaluate the veracity of using natural interfaces as a form of interaction as identified by Satava (Satava, 1993), in our surgical training system we developed a prototype where particular input methods were evaluated and compared. In designing the experiment, we wanted to evaluate the accuracy and discoverability of the input methods. The first criterion was measured by the error from an ideal target, while the second was measured by the time between starting the task and making a selection.

The experiment utilizes three different devices (mouse, glove, and Leap Motion) along with the keyboard to manipulate a virtual bar and disk used to push and pull the spherical particles of a softbody (Nvidia Flex) object in the world. The finalized softbody object was a slightly rounded cube of Flex particles.

Shared keyboard inputs for the three device interactions include the A and D keys to rotate around the model, the space bar to lock a selection and switch from selection mode to manipulation mode, and the enter key as the marker for start and stop of a task.

The A and D keys were chosen as they are the familiar and standard input navigation keys in computer games (WASD). However, the mapping is slightly different as the movement is not translational nor changing the viewport according to the user, but rather rotational around a point. The A and D keys were also chosen instead of the arrow keys because it would ease the separation between the two hands, allowing the right hand to focus on movement while the left hand focused on other selection tasks.

The space bar was chosen to maintain consistency among the different devices. Original versions of the system included different methods for locking a selection for each device. The mouse selection involved clicking and holding down the left mouse button, a standard and intuitive way of making a selection. The Leap selection utilized the pinch gesture available through UE4. However, the glove had no particular method for making a selection, since the original design utilized the flex of the fingers as the area of the selection. Because there was no method of selection for the glove, and the Leap selection gesture was unstable, the decision was made to use the spacebar as the locking mechanism for all devices.

The enter key was chosen as it was farther away from the A and D keys, requiring deliberate thought to select the beginning and end of the trial. The mouse was used specifically for training purposes, familiarising subjects with committing selections using the space bar, locating the targets, and pressing the Enter key on start and end of the task. The mouse utilized the 2D Cartesian coordinates of the mouse in the viewport and mapped the values to the pitch and yaw of the target. The glove and Leap used the roll to control the yaw, and the pitch to control the pitch of the target. The difference was that the glove used the wrist sensors located on the back of the wrist, while the Leap used the palm orientation. The effect of this is negligible as they are in approximately the same position on the hand.

A combined user study was conducted to compare the usability of contact (5DT Glove) and non-contact (the Leap) gesture-based input devices for use in the system. The combined study incorporated both User Experience and functional usability techniques. Eleven right-handed adult volunteers were recruited. Each volunteer was asked to perform four tasks on the deformable model. These tasks involved pushing and pulling certain points and faces on the 3D model.

To account for possible learning bias, subjects were randomly assigned their first device. After each device, the subjects completed a System Usability Scale questionnaire.

The experiment collected information on the (a) accuracy, (b) discoverability, and (c) ease of use of the two devices.

- Accuracy was measured based on the distance between the user's selected location and a predetermined target point.
- Discoverability was based on the time taken to reach the selection point.
- Ease of use was determined by survey.

The users were asked to complete four tasks related to virtual object manipulation. They were:
1. Push the front bottom right corner of the model
2. Pull the back top right corner of the model
3. Push the front face of the model
4. Pull the top face of the model

Subjects started with the mouse as the input method for training, and were then randomly assigned a first device by coin toss. Out of 11 subjects, six were assigned the glove first and five were assigned the Leap first.

Subjects were read a script designed to give only cursory information about how to make selections and manipulate the target; they were given very little instruction on the mechanism for using the wrist for manipulation. This was intentional as the discoverability of the method was something that we wanted to establish.

The user completed the four tasks with their first assigned device, completed a questionnaire, completed the four tasks with the other device, and then filled out the questionnaire in relation to the second device. The questionnaire was a version of the System Usability Scale, chosen for ease of evaluation and its standardization.

While the user was performing the tasks, the system was capturing the input data and writing it to a file. To measure accuracy, the pitch, yaw, and roll of the manipulation object was compared with a pre-determined ideal position. The time taken to reach this ideal position, was captured as a measure of how easy it was for the user to manipulate around the object.

The subjects were polled on whether they play video games, how many hours per week they play, and their primary mode of gaming (virtual, i.e. mobile phones; keyboard-and-mouse, i.e. PC; or console, i.e. controller).

The questions asked in the User Experience (UX) part include:
- Which is more accurate: the Glove or the Leap?
- How discoverable is movement designed to mimic the motion of the users wrist?
- Which device provides a better experience for the user?

Findings & Results

Standard descriptive statistics are employed (mainly means and standard deviations).

Discoverability

Discoverability was based on the time it took for the user to commit to a location for their selection. This measures the "playing around" time in order to achieve the goal.

The first three tasks show a preference for the glove in speed, which when taken independently of accuracy can indicate users' preference for it. Only the fourth task indicates a choice for the Leap. Figure 1 shows the four results. Note that timing should not be compared between different tasks, only within the devices for the particular task.

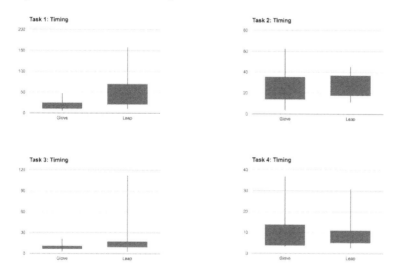

Figure 1. Spread of timing values from start to most accurate selection

As illustrated in the previous figure, Glove has better averages in all tasks except for task 4.

Comparing accuracy between the glove and the Leap (Error Rate).

The first task involved the user pushing the bottom-right corner of the model. From the results, it seems that the glove (mean of 18.37) was more accurate overall than the Leap (mean of 30.10). A possible explanation for the greater accuracy could be that the user had more freedom to move around with the glove and eventually hit the correct spot, even if the mental model was not well discoverable.

The second task involved pulling the back top-right corner of the model. Once corrected for some ambiguity in the instruction, the result is a mixed picture in which neither the Leap (mean of 6.78) nor the Glove (mean of 5.41) appears to be more accurate.

The third task involved pushing the front face of the model. Again the users were slightly better using the Glove (mean of 11.08) than they were with the Leap (mean of 16.74).

Finally, the fourth task was pulling the top face of the model. The results were comparable for the glove (mean of 49.08) and the Leap (mean of 43.76) with the Leap slightly better.

User Experience

Out of the 11 subjects, six chose the Leap as the preferable interaction method while five subjects chose the glove as the preferable method. The SUS results give a slightly different picture. The SUS results show five subjects with a preference for the glove while only four subjects prefer the Leap and two rated the two devices as equal. Additionally, the average score for the glove of those who preferred the glove is much higher than the average score for those who preferred the Leap.

Comments on preferences seem to mostly fall into the category of "device X seemed more accurate" or "device X seemed easier to use". Glove-subjects tend to describe the glove as more accurate, along with easy to use, while Leap-subjects cite ease of use more often than they mention accuracy. For those who preferred the Leap, a major factor was the limits of the glove and how clunky it felt, whether citing the glove as negative or the Leap as positive. That being said, this preference has the possibility of being eliminated as lighter and more advanced gloves are available.

We can also split users up into various demographics. Four subjects self-identified as non-gamers, three of whom preferred the Leap. Seven subjects self-identified as gamers and they were also close, with a majority toward the glove (4-3). Among the gamers, there seems to be no correlation between how long individuals play video games and their preference.

Discussion

The study undertaken comprised a small number of subjects. A greater sample size is necessary to yield results regarding any possible correlation between gaming and device usage. That said, even with a small sample size, the results highlight interesting questions. Primarily they indicate that while non-contact based devices might be perceived as having greater ease of use due to the lack of restrictions and cabling when compared to the glove, the glove was more accurate. The level of preference for the glove among those who preferred the glove was higher than the level of preference for the Leap among those who preferred the Leap.

The significance of this is dependent upon the type of learning scenario employed in the serious game. If the emphasis within the serious game is on task training, e.g. dexterous tasks associated with surgical instrument manipulation, then the results suggest the use of the Glove is more appropriate due its higher accuracy. However, if the focus in the serious game is on naturalness of interaction then the Leap is more highly preferred.

There has been relatively little research undertaken to date on this problem, despite it being identified by Schijven (Schijven, 2003) and Halvorsen (Halvorsen, 2005). This probably has more to do with the emphasis on traditional surgical instrument inputs.

These insights may help serious game designers and educational content creators in adopting the appropriate input device for natural gesture-based interaction.

Conclusion

In this study we have undertaken a preliminary evaluation of the feasibility of incorporating gesture-based natural interfaces in to a serious game. The results indicate that the non-contact gesture input device offered a more natural interaction, while the more encumbered contact gesture interaction device (glove) was more accurate.

Recommendations

We plan to further explore the suitability of these two different (contact vs non-contact) gesture based input devices in more dexterous tasks in the next version of the surgical training system. There is scope for further studies to compare the learning against more established simulation systems. We also plan to evaluate these gesture inputs with medical and surgical practionners, and finally we will have to evaluate the 'transferability' of the learning to the actual surgical procedure itself.

References

Gorman, P.J., Meier A.H., & Krummel, T.M., 2000. Computer-assisted training and learning in surgery. *Computer Aided Surgery, 5,* 120–130.

Bradley, P., 2006. The History of Simulation in Medical Education and possible future directions. *Medical Education, 40,* 254-264

Bowman, D., Kruijff, E., LaViola Jr, J.J. and Poupyrev, I.P., 2004. 3D User Interfaces: Theory and Practice, CourseSmart eTextbook. Addison-Wesley.

Murphy, D., Doherty, G., &Luz, S., 2008. Differentiating between novice and expert surgeons based on errors derived from task analysis., 15th European Conference on Cognitive Ergonomics. ACM, 32.

Pavlovic, V.I., Sharma, R. and Huang, T.S., 1997. Visual interpretation of hand gestures for human-computer interaction: A review. *IEEE Transactions on pattern analysis and machine intelligence, 19*(7), pp.677-695.

Mitra, S. and Acharya, T., 2007. Gesture recognition: A survey. *IEEE Transactions on Systems, Man, and Cybernetics, Part C (Applications and Reviews), 37*(3), pp.311-324.

Satava, R.M., 1993. Virtual reality surgical simulator. *Surgical endoscopy, 7*(3), pp.203-205.

Schijven, M. and Jakimowicz, J., 2003. Virtual reality surgical laparoscopic simulators. *Surgical Endoscopy And Other Interventional Techniques, 17*(12), pp.1943-1950.

Halvorsen, F.H., Elle, O.J. and Fosse, E., 2005. Simulators in surgery. *Minimally Invasive Therapy & Allied Technologies, 14*(4-5), pp.214-223.

Gallagher, A. G., et al., 2005, Virtual Reality Simulation for the Operating Room: Proficiency-Based Training as a Paradigm Shift in Surgical Skills Training. Annals of Surgery, 241(2), p.364

McCloy, R., Stone, R., 2001. Virtual Reality in Surgery. British Medical Journal, 323, p912.

Sliney, A., Murphy, D., 2011. Using serious games for assessment. Serious Games and Edutainment Applications. Springer London

Kneebone, R., 2003. Simulation in surgical training: Educational issues and practical implications. *Medical Education, 37*(3), 267–77.

Herndon, K.P., Van Dam, A., Gleicher, M., 1994. "The challenges of 3D interaction". ACM SIGCHI Bulletin 26(4) pp. 36–43.

Weng, S., Hsieh, C., Chu, Y., 2015. A Vision-based Virtual Keyboard Design. Intelligent Systems and Applications: Proceedings of the International Computer Symposium. pp. 641–647.

Lawrence, D., Cutler, L.D., et al., 1997. Two-handed direct manipulation on the responsive workbench. Proceedings of the 1997 symposium on Interactive 3D graphics, pp. 107–114.

LaViola, J.J., Keefe, D.F., 2011. 3D spatial interaction. ACM SIGGRAPH '11, pp. 1–75.

CHAPTER V

IMPROVISATIONAL MENTORING: A FRAMEWORK FOR
CREATIVE TEACHING IN CHARACTER-PLAYING GAMES

JENNIFER E. KILLHAM

The Need for Creative Teaching

Thriving in classrooms today requires creative teaching approaches. Yet, for early career teachers, creative expectations have been largely inaccessible. Clearer orientations on creative teaching must be established (Engelsrud, 2007; Kurtz, 2011; Sassi; 2011), especially because of the perceived contrast with the standardization movement (Fournier, 2011). However, a space where early career teachers can wrestle with the tension between classroom structure and dynamism is lacking (c.f. Beghetto and Kaufman, 2011; DeZutter, 2011).

Fortunately, games-like platforms present a playground for exploration into creative teaching capacities. This paper explores the use of a character-playing game called *Place Out of Time* (*POOT*) to develop creative teaching capacities, such as improvisational mentoring. *POOT* was selected because it has a built-in mentoring component to help pre-service teachers gain early exposure to dynamic teaching environments (Killham, 2014; Kupperman, Fahy, Goodman, Hapgood, Stanzler, & Weisserman, 2011).

A Case for Improvisation

Rigidity teaching risks "sealing off" of creative intellectualism (Beghetto and Kaufman, 2011, p. 95), whereas the structure and dynamism in improvisation offers a richer platform for creative teaching capacities. Improvisation is an "attunement to a situational context" with "spontaneous decision making" (Kurtz, 2011, p. 133). Fournier (2011) suggested, "[b]y its nature, improvisation invites surprises" (p. 184). Erickson (2011) defined improvisation as the "social action that is guided by existing structures," all the while maintaining "opportunities for choice for participants" (p. 130), a definition that balances imparting knowledge and co-constructing (Scardamalia & Bereiter (2006), as cited in Fournier, 2011, p. 204).

Improvisational mentoring (IM), akin to Sawyer's (2011) notion of creative teaching, creates a generative space between that is fluid (e.g., adaptations to the lesson or modifying rules) and planned environments (e.g., lessons or classroom rules), also described as "purposeful, but not predetermined" (Jurow & Creighton, 2005). The aim is, as Erickson stressed, to find "the right balance between structure and improvisation" (p. 131) and to develop the ability for these principles to co-exist (p. 114), a combination that can help educators to "rework fixed and fluid aspect of their curriculum to simultaneously support student learning and creative expression (Beghetto and Kaufman, 2011, p. 108).

Methods

Setting

The venue for this exploration was *Place Out of Time* (*POOT*), an online, semester-long, character-playing experience. Middle and high school teachers from around the world register their classrooms (approximately 200 participants per game). Teachers, accompanied by teaching assistants enrolled in a university mentoring seminar (i.e., mentors), engage as full participants. Adult participants are afforded additional website access in order to track the type and quantity of participation.

Participants adopt the persona of a historical figure, such as a powerful head of states (e.g., Bloody Mary of England), a heartless nobleman (Archduke Franz Ferdinand of Austria), or a warrior goddess (Athena), and conduct research about the person in order to promote an accurate portrayal.

Participants use first-person language and asynchronous text to engage in spirited discourse around controversial socio-political issues, such as the following fictional but plausible court case:

"Kadhim v. City of Stockholm, Sweden

Muhammad Kadhim, a Muslim and citizen of Sweden, petitions the Court of All Time to rule, on the authority of the Justices and Guests at the Alhambra Palace, in favor of his right to build a mosque in a downtown district of Stockholm, Sweden.

Sweden's 1991fundamental law on freedom of expression guarantees the "right of free expression, whether orally, pictorially, in writing, or in any other way" to all Swedish citizens (with certain restrictions regarding hate speech against any group based on ethnicity, race, creed or sexual orientation).

Following a terrorist bombing carried out by Muslim extremists that caused considerable damage in Stockholm in fall 2010, an injunction was imposed on the building of a mosque, already under construction, that was designed by, and was being built under the supervision of Mr. Kadhim's firm.

Mr. Kadhim is asking the Court of All Time to render a judgment in favor of his right to continue with the construction of the mosque. Opponents to the mosque argue that following the horrible events of last fall, it would be insensitive and provocative to build a mosque within blocks of where the recent attack took place.

A ruling of "yes" would side with Mr. Kadhim's petition to resume the building of the mosque. A ruling of "no" would uphold the injunction."

Participants are requested to spend a minimum of two hours on the site per week. Behind the scenes, university mentors are paired up with K-12 students. Mentors serve as thought provocateurs that guide deeper learning (Killham, Tyler, Venable, Raider-Roth, 2014). However, mentors are bound to the same set of rules, requiring mentorship to occur in-character. Students know that there are mentors sharing the virtual space but do are not required to engage with them in a traditional teacher-student dynamic. Participants have a choice on with whom they converse; therefore, mentors need to consider authentic engagement techniques as they attempt to reach out to the mentee.

Large group discussions are facilitated through public posts made by a "host" character, the adult serving as the master of ceremony. Start-up questions include, "What objects do you value to the virtual meeting space?" The game's facilitator guides conversation towards more complicated geopolitical issues, ranging from immigration, tolerance, and freedoms. An example questions include, "Does banning a veiled 14-year old Muslim girl from public school on the basis of a dress code violation support separation of church and state, respect for religious freedom, and individual expression?"

Procedures

Qualitative teacher-action research (Cochran-Smith & Lytle, 2009) guided this three-year participatory field experience. The aim was to co-construct a theory around creative teaching capacities in character-playing games because earlier research revealed that creative teaching in *POOT* was not intuitive (Killham, 2014). University mentors struggled with interactions with students who did not conform to the general guidelines of the game or had minimal participation. . Participants were 119 *POOT* mentor characters portrayed by university students at two large Schools of Education, as well as 28 facilitator characters portrayed by classroom teachers. Seidel's (1998) method of learning through looking and Glanz's (1998) cycle of acting, observing, and reflecting were central to data collection and analysis. The lead researchers participated as both *POOT* characters and action researchers, each compiling research memos about observations. Members of the interpretive community had a strong working knowledge of *POOT* and teacher education. Data included archived public and private postings on the *POOT* website, Blackboard posts, blogs entries, post-simulation reflection papers, course evaluations, as well as six semi-structured interviews.

Results

The improvisational mentor is tasked with (re)considering how to orchestrate authentic learning connections within asynchronous text-based conversations. Developing the capacity to do this requires naming the desired dispositions mentors should embody. Through thematic analysis of the data, four pedagogical principles were derived: (a) responsive interactivity, (b) a disposition of care, (c) nuanced pedagogical initiatives, and (d) authentic feedback loop.

Responsive Interactivity

Responsive interactivity emphasizes a heightened awareness to relational and situational attunement, which promotes discovering one's own voice, inviting surprise, and venturing off in unexpected directions through an emergent script. Further, encouraging students to speak freely is essential (Kurtz, 2011, p. 156). Overly scripted settings should be avoided because it restricts learners, essentially placing limits on intellectual maneuverability (Sawyer, 2000, p. 138). Instead, actions should spark "collective creativeness" (Sawyer, 2000, p. 155) a term associated with creative teaching. Allowing "young people to define or respond to issues in ways that resonate with them and their friends, shape their ideas, amplify their voices, and heighten their influence" (Cohen & Kahne, 2012, p. 4) is a critical dimension to the work of the mentor.

A Disposition of Care

Embodying a disposition of care strengthens the ongoing authentic learning partnership, something students identified as important in program evaluations (c.f. "I loved how I was able to meet new people and build new relationships"). Relationships should be growth enhancing, meaning adopting a strength seeking stance as opposed to deficit thinking. The relationship should evolve based on the interactivity between players. Through the lens of character-play, mentors need to build trust with the other players and to see the younger participants as intellectual partners (Fournier, 2011, p. 202). Attending to the complete context of the learning partnership assists with this process.

Nuances Pedagogical Initiatives

In addition to the interactivity described above, improvisation "depends on structure – it works within it" and it "takes advantage of aspect of pattern in order to create new patterns" such as "opportunistic use of structure points" which can lead to "meaningful variations" (Erickson, 2011, pp. 113-114). Character-playing games such as *POOT* enable the kind of flexibility necessary to promote creative pedagogical moves while simultaneously offering structure. The *POOT* design provides structure (e.g., the scenario for the court case), predictability (e.g., messages are posted by a host at the start of the week in the announcement section), and boundaries (e.g., you must speak in character while on the *POOT* interface). Additional, part of the work of a mentor is to make judgments about when to intervene with curricular scaffolding. Skillfully timed interventions are especially important with the introduction of primary sources and promotion of historical accuracy. To assist with interventions, mentors should pause to engage in Deweyian style reflective thinking (Rogers, 2002), what Martin and Towers (2011) call a "sophisticated capacity to step back" (p. 275). During this (active) pause, mentors ask themselves what the student and the scenario needs most.

Authentic Feedback Loop

Character-playing games are a intellectually challenging platform for re-envisioning of notions of success and failure. This principles takes the position that multiple solutions to a "problem" are possible (Goodman, 2010). Not every problem has a scripted solution. Failure (e.g., a character recited a date wrong in a posting) is viewed differently than in traditional school (e.g., a mentor can provide corrective feedback through various means). Beghetto and Kaufman (2011) urged teachers to "let students know when their contributions are not making sense" (p. 106), as well as to "provide the kind of evaluative feedback that attempts to encourage student expression and also stresses how students might improve" (p. 106). This can be a form of micro-feedback (e.g., a response to a student played character's comment in *POOT*) or feedback on a larger scale (e.g., end of program reflection journal). It is essential to reposition the student from consumer to co-producer and ask the student to carry some responsibility for the assessment process. Students are also providing mentors with feedback, emphasizing that feedback is multi-directional.

Practical Implications

Below are several exchanges taking place with the character Matt Groening. The reader should puzzle over the posts, considering how they might intervene applying improvisational mentoring. The student portraying Matt Groening was chosen as an example because the university mentoring seminar puzzled over his posts.

Excerpt from Matt Groening's profile:
"Hi, my full name is Matthew Abraham Groening. I grew up in Portland, Oregon, and my parents names are Homer P. Groening, and Margaret Ruth... At the moment, I am right as rain. I like to be like my character Homer and say "D'oh!" often. In my pockets I have my lucky pen and a little scratch pad. An annoying habit I have is stopping in the middle of conversations and scribbling down ideas. My childhood was fantastic, but I always hated school. I have a college education, but most of my skills are natural... One of my greatest hobbies is drawing (Duh). My most treasured possession besides my family is my hands. My idea of good entertainment is cartoons. Good jokes usually make me laugh. If I had insomnia, I would just stay up doodling (I sometimes do that now!) I deal with stress by using stress balls."

Matt Groening's legal philosophy:
"I am so psyched that I have been chosen to be a justice. I am not very experienced in this, but I will do my best. I feel that no one person should make a law, but a whole group. If a large number of people in a city are continously pressing a problem, then they should have the right to create a law that would solve the problem. I think laws should be applied to everybody, but there are always exceptions. If the president is speeding to get to a meeting, he will not get pulled over and given a ticket. (No offense Obama.) If there is a disagreement about a law, I think the public should decide again. I feel that not everybody is entitled to the same privileges. You have to earn everything you get, not just get it handed to you. I feel that a justice is someone who voices the public. (The jury, in this case.)"

Angela Davis wrote,
"I read your legal philosophy...I agree with you on many of your perspectives but however I have some questions to help understand some of your points .. You say that everyone is not all titled to the same privileges and you have to earn everything you get, it should not be handed to you. What do you mean by that? Do you not believe in equal justice under the law? Do you not think everyone should receive the same treatment in a court of law? If so, I disagree. I do not believe that anyone should be a victim of discrimination, especially in the court of law. Lastly Matt I was wondering what you feel the main responsibility of a justice is? What is your obligation to the people? If you had to sum up in one sentence your legal philosophy in terms of your responsibilities and obligations, what would that one sentence be?"

Matt Groening replied,
"Dear Angela, I am so very sorry for not responding to you faster. It has been ages since I last got hold of a computer. I had push a hippie of his Mac at Starbucks just so I could send this to you. I have been on the run lately, and I will answer your intriguing questions some other time. The hippie is starting to fight back now. a;sldkfjal;sidhgfp oa;dfighja ;lsdijfa ;lks;dolfj a;sldkfjsincerely, Masa;ltija;lkshtjak;lsdhjfa;lsdkjttttaslktjttt"

Consider what the best next step should be through the lens of improvisational mentoring. Also give consideration the next step from a variety of perspectives (i.e., a politician, social activist, religious figure, scientist, and celebrity) throughout times past.

Conclusion

Pre-service teachers require access to spaces, such as character-playing games, which can help them develop an ethic of care (i.e., capacity to see the good in learners) over an ethic of justice (i,e., deficit thinking). Four themes emerged as central to the development of creative teaching capacities for mentors using a character-playing experience. While enacting the themes, mentors should intentionally pause. The pause permits consideration for what next steps will foster of deep learning. Character-playing games are a powerful means to assist more skilled others (i.e., teachers and pre-service teachers in mentoring roles) with the internalization of students as a knowledge generators, strengthening an ethic of care, recognizing multiple solutions are possible, and supporting improvisational attunement.

Acknowledgements

Thank you to Jeff Kupperman, Jeff Stanzler, and Michael Fahy at the University of Michigan's Interactive Communications and Simulations Group, Covenant Foundation, and the University of Cincinnati's Center for Studies in Jewish Education and Culture for supporting this research. Heartfelt appreciation is extended to the Institute of Innovation in Education, a well as the Action Women, Action Figures, Kelli Jette, Peggy Shannon-Baker, Stephanie Talbot, Gail Headley, and Khahlia Sanders for their insight into earlier iterations of improvisational mentoring.

References

Beghetto, R. A. & Kaufman, J. C., 2011. Improvising Within the System: Creating New Teacher Performances in inner City Schools. In Sawyer, R. K., Ed., 2011. Structure and improvisation in creative teaching. Cambridge University Press.

Cochran-Smith, M. & Lytle, S.L., 2009. Inquiry as stance. New York: Teachers College Press.

Cohen, C. J., & Kahne, J., 2012. Participatory Politics: New Media and Youth Political Action. MacArthur Foundation.

DeZutter, S., 2011. Professional Improvisation and Teacher Education: Opening the Conversation. In Sawyer, R. K., Ed., 2011. Structure and improvisation in creative teaching. Cambridge: Cambridge University Press.

Engelsrud, G., 2007. Teaching Styles in Contact Improvisation: An Explicit Discourse with Implicit Meaning, Dance Research Journal, Vol. 39, No. 2 (Winter, 2007), pp. 58-73

Erickson, F., 2011. Taking Advantage of Structure to Improvise in instruction: Examples from Elementary School Classrooms. In Sawyer, R. K., Ed., 2011. Structure and improvisation in creative teaching. Cambridge: Cambridge University Press.

Fournier, J. E., 2011. Productive Improvisation and Collective Creativity: Lessons from the Dance Studio. In Sawyer, R. K., Ed., 2011. Structure and improvisation in creative teaching. Cambridge: Cambridge University Press.

Glanz, J., 1998. Action Research: An educational leader's guide to school improvement. Norwood: Christopher-Gordon Publishers.

Goodman, F., 2010, June. Essay: Games, gods, and grades. THEN Journal. [online] Avilable at http://thenjournal.org/index.php/then/article/view/46/45; [Accessed 17 June, 2017].

Jurow, A., & Creighton, L., 2005. Improvisational science discourse: Teaching science in two K-1 classrooms. Linguistics & Education, 16(3), pp. 275-297.

Killham, J., 2014. Exploring the Affordances of Role in the Online History Education Project "Place Out of Time:" A Narrative Analysis. PhD dissertation, viewed 12 December, 2016, Electronic Theses and Dissertation Center.

Killham, J., Tyler, S. P., Venable, A., Raider-Roth, M., 2014. Mentoring in an Online Simulation: Shaping Preservice Teachers for Tomorrow's Roles. Teaching & Learning: The Journal of Natural Inquiry and Reflective Practice, 28(2), pp. 62-79

Kupperman, J., Fahy, M., Goodman, F. Hapgood, S., Stanzler, J. & Weisserman, G., 2011. It matters because it's a game: Serious games and serious players. International Journal of Learning and Media, 2(4), pp. 21-30.

Kurtz, J., 2011. Breaking Through the Communicative Cocoon: Improvisation in Secondary School Foreign Language Classrooms. In Sawyer, R. K., Ed., 2011. Structure and improvisation in creative teaching. Cambridge: Cambridge University Press.

Martin, L. C., & Towers, J., 2011. Improvisational understanding in the mathematics classroom. In Sawyer, R. K., Ed., 2011. Structure and improvisation in creative teaching. Cambridge: Cambridge University Press.

Rodgers, C., 2002. Defining reflection: Another look at John Dewey and reflective thinking, New York: Teachers College Record, 104(4), pp. 842–866.

Sassi, A., 2011. How 'scripted' materials might support improvisational teaching: insights from the implementation of a reading comprehension curriculum. In Sawyer, R. K., Ed. (2011). Structure and improvisation in creative teaching. Cambridge University Press.

Sawyer, R. K., Ed., 2011. Structure and improvisation in creative teaching. Cambridge University Press.

Seidel, S., 1998. Learning from looking. With portfolio in hand. New York: Teachers College Press, pp. 69-89.

CHAPTER VI

USING GAMIFICATION TO PROMOTE EFFECTIVE TIME-MANAGEMENT IN TERTIARY EDUCATION

TRACEY CASSELLS

Introduction

At the beginning of the academic year, tertiary institutions may encourage new students to spend their initial time setting out a study plan (NUI Galway, 2016). However while students enter college with the expectation that they will effectively manage their time, other academic pressures interfere and can deter them from investing their time into long-term planning.

Time-management is defined by Claessens as "*behaviors that aim at achieving an effective use of time while performing certain goal-directed activities*" (Claessens, Eerde, Rutte and Roe, 2007). Students use time-management to help estimate study times, to sufficiently plan for tests and deadlines, and to set priorities (Chickering and Gamson, 1987; Meer, Jansen and Torenbeek, 2010). Placing an early emphasis on time-management can reduce students' stress and aid in student retention and can teach students to prioritize important tasks, improve their time-estimates, break up complex tasks and maintain a structured routine (Kornhauser, 1993; García-Ros, Pérez-González and Hinojosa, 2004).

The efforts of institutions however can be hindered by students' perception that managing one's time is not an inherently engaging task. Students may be unwilling to invest their time into tasks that benefit their long-term goals, if they perceive the task as mundane (Steel, 2007). To address this problem and make time-management more engaging we are investigating gamification, the use of game elements in non game contexts (Marczewski, 2013).

Gamification

Gamification is classed as the "*application of gaming metaphor to real life tasks to influence behavior, improve motivation and enhance engagement*" by (Marczewski, 2013). The inclusion of game elements has been found to increase engagement in areas such as health, sport, business, education and the formation of daily habits (Hamari, Koivisto and Sarsa, 2014). Previous studies into the use of gamification in education shows tertiary level students respond positively to the inclusion of game elements in academic learning (O'Donovan, Gain and Marais, 2013). Paisley (2013) found a significant increase in students' perceived engagement as well as an increase in their perceived motivation with the implementation of gamification. Applied correctly gamification has been seen to promote positive behaviour, increase cognition in learning and create a stronger connection between students and their education (Appleton, Christenson, Kim and Reschly, 2006).

While gamification has the potential to help optimise productivity there it has seen little exploration of its use in time-management so far (Hamari, Koivisto and Sarsa, 2014). As gamification is a relatively recent concept, there is at present, a shortfall of gamified time-management applications specifically designed for students. This scarcity needs to be addressed as there is evidence to suggest such an application would be successful in engaging students (Claessens et al., 2007).

This study aims to address this shortfall and answer the question *"can gamification help promote and optimise time management for students in tertiary education?"*.

Process

To answer this question a gamified study planner application was proposed and the Design Thinking (DT) process from Stanford's Human Computer Interaction (HCI) course was utilized (Stanford, 2016). The DT process is an iterative design methodology built around identifying the user's needs when creating a product. This design process consists of five stages Empathy, Define, Ideate, Prototype and Test. These stages are repeated as necessary, with multiple iterations of the process helping to narrow the scope.

For the empathy stage we analyzed the responses from a self-report online survey that had been given to computer and business students within the college. The initial survey questions focused on the respondent's perception of their time-management, their study habits and their use of tools to assist with time-management. The latter part of the survey focused specifically on the use of online-study planner apps, why they may or may not be used and what features would be desirable in such an application. This survey was followed by a series of ten minute intercept interviews to garner a more detailed description of a student's use of time-management tools and to identify any pain points not found in previous interviews.

51 students responded to the questionnaire, in general respondents felt they needed better time-management with 68% of respondents responding "I would like to manage my time more effectively" and only 26% of respondents feeling confident that they were managing their time well. Time estimation was a problem for many respondents with only 30% feeling confident in their time estimates; 44% felt they could not estimate a task well if they had not completed it before. Less than a third of respondents planned out their activities for the day beforehand with only 43% feeling that most of the activities they completed in a college day had some purpose.

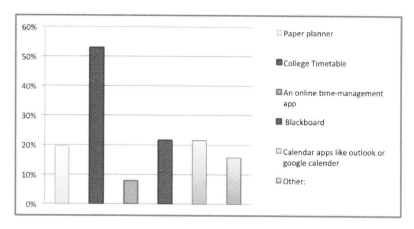

Table 1: Different tools used by students to manage their time

Respondents used few tools to help in structuring their time as shown in Table 1. Over 58% of respondents had never used a study planner before with 31% never considering using one before now. A similar study by the University of Southampton found 43.7% of students used software to aid in their time-management, 35.6% used pen and paper, while 29.9% of students used no time-management tools at all (Rebenich, Gravell and Tiropanis, 2010).

In the section relating to what features students would like to see in a time-management application the features most selected were reminders for deadlines, prioritizing tasks by importance and notification of class changes [Table 2].

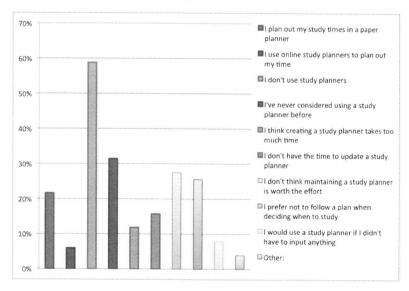

Table 2: Students' attitudes towards study planners

A similar study by the University of Southampton found 55.7% of students use calendaring software on their mobile devices (Rebenich, Gravell and Tiropanis, 2010). Of these students, 43.7%

used software to aid in time-management, 35.6% used pen and paper, while 29.9% of students used no time-management tools at all [Table 3]. The aspects of time–management tools the students considered of the most importance were, considering deadlines, estimating task times and size and setting priorities (Rebenich, Gravell and Tiropanis, 2010).

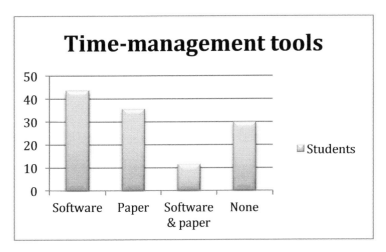

Table 3: The different technologies used by students at Southampton (Rebenich, Gravell and Tiropanis, 2010).

Following the online-questionnaire students were asked if they would be willing to participate in a short five-minute interview. The response rate was low, with 15 participants agreeing. Interview questions related to how they managed their time, the tools they used, their perceived control of time, the accuracy of their time-estimates and their largest concerns about completing work on time. The interviewed students largely followed the trend from the questionnaire of not using tools to manage their time. Some of the interviewees would set themselves reminders using sticky notes and lists. Topics that arose that were not covered in the questionnaire included an inability to complete work due to tiredness and difficulties at home distracting from college work. Concerns not related to time-management were also raised, with the majority of interviewed students mentioning confusion from vague instructions. There were also concerns about deadlines clashing; deadlines were often extended and one student mentioned they preferred if they were not giving extensions as it affected other projects. In general students felt they were not managing their time well and did not have enough control over their time.

Define

After empathizing/need-finding the problem statement was defined:

"students find it difficult to estimate the time a task will take, it can be difficult to gauge the time a new task will take and lecturer estimates are not always accurate, planning and setting priorities can be affected by fluctuating time-estimates and project deadlines. An uncertain and inefficient use of time by both students and lecturers can affect a students' health and engagement with their course".

Once the problem was defined, various solutions and features were considered during ideation, including features suggested by the students during the empathising stage. As part of Ideation other time-management systems were assessed. Current popular study planner apps available to students such as MyStudyApp (My Study Life, 2016) are strictly task management systems and do not utilize game elements. Time-management applications utilizing gamification such as Doable (Trello, 2016) and Habitica (Habitica, 2016) are focused on task completion and do not address the need for time-estimates. More similar to the proposed system is Wimble (MeKiwi, 2014) a kickstarter app that uses game elements such as customization, badges and level progression to help users organize their time. However this application is still limited in scope and is not applicable to student specific needs. Following the Ideation stage a prototype design was created.

Design

Prototyping saw the creation of a study-planner as a cross-platform web application, accessible using both mobile devices and desktop or laptop computers. The planner contains student activities for the upcoming school semester including class times, deadlines and study hours.

In the study-planner prototype colored blocks detailing the class titles and times represent the activities, examples of which can be seen in Figure 1. Time restricted activities such as tests and project deadlines are shown in red and rest on their own tier. Once a lecturer adds a new project or test date to the planner the system will automatically assign study hours for the project/test based on free time available and the lecturers' estimation of study hours needed. Students can modify these hours in their own time and these readjustments will be noted by the systems algorithm to aid future estimations.

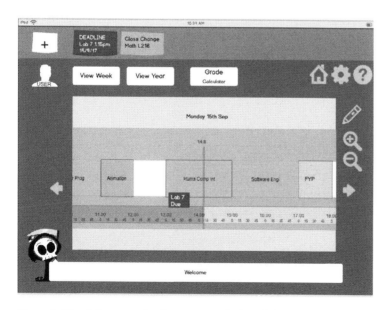

Figure 1: The daily screen for the prototype design of the system

When a study hour is reached a notification is sent to the student, they will then have the option to start, postpone or decline. Postponing will set the study hour to a new free hour while declining will freeze it, once the hour is up the student receives another notification asking if they are now finished. By getting responses through notifications the system can update itself without waiting on the user, in turn removing the drudgery of maintaining a study planner For the proposed system multiple game elements are currently in consideration including traditional points, badge and leaderboards (PBL), customization, personalized stats, betting, competition and chance.

Methodology

The study planner will be used in a within-subjects study across a number of modules in a third-level computing course throughout the 2017/2018 academic year. Data will be collected through the students' interaction with the system and response rates to reminders.

Feedback will be collected from focus groups, semi-structured interviews and questionnaires. Instruments include time-management questionnaires such as the time structure questionnaire (TSQ) by Bond & Feather(1988) and time management questionnaire (TMQ) by Britton and Tesser (1991). Quantitative data stored will include any changes to the study planner as well as the participants' frequency of use, responses to notifications and use of individual game elements. For qualitative data participants will fill out pre and post questionnaires to determine their attitudes towards time-management, their engagement with the application and the usability of the system. From analyzing this data we can then track the different degrees of effectiveness of gamification in promoting the applications use, and the effect the app has on students' studying routines and goal setting.

Future Work

Having identified the students' needs, and outlined the design of the prototype the next step is to implement a working build for students to use over the coming school year. After addressing student concerns regarding time-management and identifying effective gamification elements, we are aiming to deploy a fully tested application for the 2017/2018 academic year. We will use this application to test the effect of gamification in motivating time-management for tertiary students, answering questions such as

- Did students find the gamified system more engaging than alternatives?
- Which individual elements did students find engaging?
- Did the application motivate them to complete their tasks on time?
- Did the application change their cognitive attitudes towards time-management?

It is hoped that through the use of this study planner we will aid students in their time-management, help reduce stress and improve performance. From the results of this study we aim to fill the current gap of gamified time-management in academic literature and increase understanding of the effects of gamification in promoting effective time-management.

References

Appleton, J.J., Christenson, S.L., Kim, D. and Reschly, A.L., 2006. Measuring cognitive and psychological engagement: Validation of the Student Engagement Instrument. *Journal of School Psychology*, 44(5), pp.427–445.

Bond, M.J. and Feather, N.T., 1988. Some correlates of structure and purpose in the use of time. *Journal of Personality and Social Psychology*, 55, pp.321–329.

Britton, B.K. and Tesser, A., 1991. Effects of time-management practices on college grades. *Journal of Educational Psychology*, 83(3), pp.405–410.

Chickering, A.W. and Gamson, Z.F., 1987. Seven Principles for Good Practice in Undergraduate Education. *AAHE Bulletin*. [online] Available at: <http://eric.ed.gov/?id=ED282491> [Accessed 14 Jul. 2016].

Claessens, B.J.C., Eerde, W. van, Rutte, C.G. and Roe, R.A., 2007. A review of the time management literature. *Personnel Review*, 36(2), pp.255–276.

García-Ros, R., Pérez-González, F. and Hinojosa, E., 2004. Assessing Time Management Skills as an Important Aspect of Student Learning The Construction and Evaluation of a Time Management Scale with Spanish High School Students. *School Psychology International*, 25(2), pp.167–183.

Habitica, 2016. *Habitica: Your Life the Role Playing Game*. [online] Habitica. Available at: <https://habitica.com/static/front> [Accessed 22 Sep. 2016].

Hamari, J., Koivisto, J. and Sarsa, H., 2014. Does Gamification Work? – A Literature Review of Empirical Studies on Gamification. In: *2014 47th Hawaii International Conference on System Sciences*. 2014 47th Hawaii International Conference on System Sciences. pp.3025–3034.

Kornhauser, A.W., 1993. *How to Study: Suggestions for High-School and College Students*. 3 edition ed. Chicago: University of Chicago Press.

Marczewski, A., 2013. *Gamification: A Simple Introduction*. Andrzej Marczewski.

Meer, J. van der, Jansen, E. and Torenbeek, M., 2010. 'It's almost a mindset that teachers need to change': first-year students' need to be inducted into time management. *Studies in Higher Education*, 35(7), pp.777–791.

MeKiwi, 2014. *Wimble - Experience Gamified, Social and Fun Time Management*. [online] Available at: <http://wimble.me/> [Accessed 23 Sep. 2016].

My Study Life, 2016. *My Study Life*. [online] mystudylife. Available at: <https://www.mystudylife.com/> [Accessed 30 Jul. 2016].

NUI Galway, 2016. *Guide to Study Skills - NUI Galway*. [online] Available at: <http://library.nuigalway.ie/support/training/usefulguides/guidetostudyskills/> [Accessed 22 Sep. 2016].

O'Donovan, S., Gain, J. and Marais, P., 2013. A Case Study in the Gamification of a University-level Games Development Course. In: *Proceedings of the South African Institute for Computer Scientists and Information Technologists Conference*, SAICSIT '13. [online] New York, NY, USA: ACM, pp.242–251. Available at: <http://doi.acm.org/10.1145/2513456.2513469> [Accessed 25 May 2015].

Paisley, V., 2013. Gamification of tertiary courses : an exploratory study of learning and engagement. *North Ryde, NSW : Macquarie University*. [online] Available at: <http://minerva.mq.edu.au:8080/vital/access/manager/Repository/mq:29904> [Accessed 5 May 2015].

Rebenich, T., Gravell, A. and Tiropanis, T., 2010. *Survey of Students' Technology Use for Time Management*. [conference] Available at: <http://eprints.soton.ac.uk/270912/> [Accessed 11 Oct. 2016].

Stanford, 2016. *Human Computer Interaction Design*. [online] Available at: <http://hci.stanford.edu/courses/cs147/2016/au/#> [Accessed 7 Feb. 2017].

Steel, P., 2007. The nature of procrastination: A meta-analytic and theoretical review of quintessential self-regulatory failure. *Psychological Bulletin*, 133(1), pp.65–94.

Trello, 2016. *doable - Stop Planning, Start Doing*. [online] Available at: <http://doableapps.com> [Accessed 22 Sep. 2016].

CHAPTER VII

REVEALING INTERACTIONS: SITUATED PLAY FOR FIRST-HAND KNOWLEDGE

ILARIA MARIANI AND VALERIA QUIRCIO

Introduction

This chapter describes the idea beyond *Noar*, a persuasive urban game designed to enquire if and how players can get affected by a game experience aimed at subverting common patterns of interaction, triggering reflections about usual or unusual social interactions. In particular: *Can it increase players' awareness of a topic of social matter as anxiety? Can we push social interactions via in-game mechanics for impacting on players, creating or increasing understanding?*

The game aims at involving players into a story of transformation, where they are not spectators who watch and empathise with the characters portrayed. They become actors in the story who can directly put themselves to the test, overturning their way of experiencing interactions. Tackling the fundamental issue of how individuals relate to their surroundings and to others, *Noar* intends to start a game-based process of change, which fundamentals are rooted in situated transformational learning theory (Mezirow, 1996). This game is indeed designed to challenge our ordinary way of perceiving and experiencing social interactions, and suggests consequential meaning making.

Literature review

Capitalizing on the considerable and multidisciplinary literature examining the relation between games and learning, between learning ecologies and gaming literacies (Gee, 2004; Salen, 2008), we explored games as cultural systems where meaningful interactions can happen, triggering comprehension and critical awareness. As Gee (2003, p.43) explained discussing games as educational models, good games should "encourage and facilitate active and critical learning and thinking". Especially over the past decade, moving beyond being mere sources of fun and entertainment, games have more and more become spaces wherein the human range of experiences and social issues can be represented and explored (Schrier and Gibson, 2010). Through a wise combination of game-structure, game-world and gameplay, designers crafted games aimed at activating critical play, asking players to alter and reconsider their way to perceive the specific issue addressed, and change their point of view accordingly. These games become powerful spaces of opportunity wherein players can learn, question and rethink their own attitudes. From a communication design perspective, their transformative potential is tied to their expressive power as persuasive systems, a topic largely discussed by seminal authors over the years. If Bogost (2007) vetted their ability to procedurally mount arguments that invite players to form judgments accordingly, scholars such as Sicart (2011), or Flanagan and Kaufman (2015; and Seidman, 2016) brought attention to the way players subjectively receive and respond to the game. Digital games as *September 12th* (Frasca, 2003), *Papers, Please* (Lucas Pope, 2013), *Gone Home* (Gaynor, 2013), and *This War of Mine* (11 bit studios, 2014) are seminal examples.

Recognizing the function of undergoing situated experiences and embodied interactions, beyond the interaction among the player and the game rules, its narrative and challenges, we focused on the relevant understanding that first-person, hands-on situated experiences can produce. Albeit their form and nature is closer to the one of events and performances, situated games as *&maybetheywontkillyou*[1] (RainBros, 2015), *Waiting Room*[2] (Pozzi and Zimmerman, 2016), and *New Atlantis*[3] (Chaos League, 2017) result able to physically immerse players into the situation portrayed through the game. Especially such an immersion can potentially affect players in a way that lasts even after the game ends (Antonacci, Bertolo and Mariani, 2017).

In the light of this reasoning, at Politecnico di Milano, Design Department, we developed *Noar*. It is a persuasive urban game that problematizes and deepens the awareness on a contemporary and timely social issue that is often underestimated: anxiety and its different aspects.

However, acknowledging the potentially harmful consequences of applying a design philosophy that privileges an ostensibly straight depiction of basics, facts and situations (Flanagan and Kaufman, 2015), the focus is shifted from acquiring specific in-game information, to acquire experience-based knowledge.

Noar challenges our ordinary conventions and bends players' ordinary behaviours and patterns of interactions. By translating anxiety symptoms and effects into game mechanics, it pushes players to have a first-hand, game-mediated experience of what it means being in the shoes of people who suffer of social anxiety.

Methods

Applying a *stealth approach* (Kaufman, Flanagan and Seidman, 2016) and including situated experiences that are source of *frustration* and *awkwardness*, *Noar* embeds persuasive messages in its mechanics and dynamics. In particular, using metaphors, this game leads players to find out for themselves what it means to fall prey to anxiety and its expressions, and how it can be binding and critical. For example, the feeling of oppression is conveyed using cellophane to bound players' arms and limit their ability to move; mutism and difficulties with verbal or physical expression become a handkerchief used as a gag that prevents the communication between members of the same team; separation anxiety is turned into a bond that ties players' ankles (Figure 1).

---

[1] http://boingboing.net/2015/08/05/carry-the-frustration-of-injus.html [Accessed 14 May 2017].

[2] https://killscreen.com/articles/waiting-rooms-is-a-building-sized-game-about-the-struggles-of-bureacracy [Accessed 14 May 2017].

[3] http://atlantisradio.org [Accessed 14 May 2017].

Figure 1: Players facing some game task.

Players undergo situated experiences that cause physical and spatial restrictions: players got impeded in their movements throughout the space, and their access is limited to specific game areas. The game was conceived following a player-centric design approach, and the iterative design methodology. Since it seeks to influence and change players' opinions raising awareness and transfer knowledge, its effectiveness is a matter of investigation.

How did players receive and perceive the game? Which sense did they make and which meanings did they grasp out of the game mechanics and narrative? To answer these key points, verifying the validity of the designer's expectations, we conducted a mixed method enquiry. The reasoning that follows comes from a singular game session that we consider an interesting synthesis of the diverse attitudes and practices observed up to now.

Held in 2016, the game session involved a sample of 8 participants (m:1, f: 7; average 24) and was investigated via rapid ethnography (Millen, 2000) and shadowing (Sclavi, 2003; McDonald, 2005), questionnaires (pre- and post-experience), and a focus group (Figure 2). Rapid ethnography and shadowing were fundamental to observe in-game behaviours. Pre- and post- experience questionnaires were built to evaluate the play(er) experience, the impact of the unusual interactions and the effectiveness of the message conveyed. Through questionnaires we also investigated the depth of each player' awareness on anxiety, identifying how this game influences it. Semi-structured focus group helped us to investigate what did players learn and how they interpret the game experience.

Finding and results

The enquiry showed that the mechanics and dynamics used by *Noar* induced a meaningful sense of frustration (Juul, 2013; Mariani, 2016), since players find out how actions they consider given for granted as normal and ordinary can become arduous (Mariani and Gandolfi, 2016) (100% high-medium – i.e., 3 or 2 on a 0 to 3 scale).

Figure 2: Players filling post-experience questionnaire, and then taking part in the focus group.

Especially interactions with other people, usually ruled by defined attitudes and implicit norms, become awkward sources of embarrassment and – sometimes, to someone – even distress (100% high-medium values – i.e., 3 or 2 on a 0 to 3 scale). To stimulate reflection on social anxiety, players were asked to distance from their ordinary attitudes and their comfort zone. Dynamic particularly effective: more than 87% of players rated it high-medium, affirming that they felt stimulated to reflection (i.e., 4 or 5 on the Likert scale) learning something (i.e., 4 or 5 on the Likert Scale).

Conducting the ethnographic observation, we noticed that players were afraid of discovering the obstacles that the game included in its quests, that are the physical metaphors of social anxiety symptoms.

First, they were nervous, then surprised and distressed to find out that to progress in the game they had to cooperate doing awkward and unusual things. For example, the solo-task that represents the sense of oppression that comes from panic attacks required players to find game elements having torso and arms bound with cellophane. This task created an evident sense of embarrassment, due to the fact that passersby could see them acting weirdly. In consequence, they often choose to ask other players for help during their walking-around activity, lessening the feeling of being alone. During the focus group, players who ran into such task said they were quiet ashamed. They also affirmed that accomplishing the collection of elements was pretty difficult. Therefore, this task resulted an effective translation of the specific symptom. Another task, representing the problem of expressing themselves, originated several communication issues within the team. After the game, players commented that they were failing in communicating and being not understood caused severe annoyance. However, they also added that once they succeed in making themselves understood, they felt proud and fiero. In addition, they stressed that being unable to speak was a source of anger. Vetting the duo-task of being bonded together with another person (tying one player's ankle to the ankle of another player), that represents the separation anxiety, it resulted that players were filled with unease. The task has been described as a significant physical contact, as an invasion of their personal space. Rather than being disturbed because they were impeded in their movements, they complained the fact of being physically stuck together with another person. Especially when it happened between players who didn't know before starting the game, this was perceived as "pesky" and "invasive".

As a matter of fact, players confirmed that they felt led to transgress established standard of behaviours, above all interpersonal .

However, the focus group and questionnaires revealed that the game succeeded in becoming a "safer space" wherein players could experience in-game subversion, feeling put to the test (more than 85 % high- medium values- i.e., 2 or 3 on a 0 to 3 scale), being questioned about their usual interpersonal interactions, and having their comfort zone challenged – in some cases also deeply.

A further level of meaning is added by the fact that the play activity takes place in the real urban space, where passersby can see and even create judgements about what is happening (Sicart, 2014; Mariani and Spallazzo, in-press). Accordingly, it became significant to explore the boundaries between what is play and what is not (Bateson, 1956; Sicart, 2014), as well as to vet the distance between manifest performance and its implicit meanings (Schechner, 1981; Turner, 1982; Mariani, 2016). This can indeed be seen again a source of *resilience*, since it brings players to a deeper self-awareness of being able to face and overcome obstacles.

Discussion

Involving players in situated experiences that use metaphors to physically translate what it means suffering from anxiety into game actions, *Noar* resulted able to activates critical experience-based reflection. Speaking of narrative aspects, the results we collected are then in line with the ones advanced by Flanagan and Kaufman (2015). The game *stealthly* embedded contents meant to provoke experiences that increase understanding and awareness in a fashion that avoids players to raise biases, as well as psychological and emotional defenses. In particular, we noticed that filling the questionnaire and debating during the focus group boosted additional reflection, leading to further trigger reflection and unpack the game's intended message. Focusing on particular aspects of the game invited players to further interpret and unpack their experiences, leading to grasp additional meaning to their previous knowledge, and sense out of their actions.

Extending the reasoning to a social perspective, players have been pushed not only to establish new and unusual interactions with other players, but also to go through uncomfortable situations and make first-hand experience of social interactions for most of them out of the ordinary.

This led to ruminate about the existant implicit and explicit rules of conduct (Anolli, 2011) that characterise the social context wherein the game takes place. In this sense, the play activity generated went beyond being just *play within a formal structure* (the game one), becoming a way to *play with structures*, celebrating experimentation. In transferring knowledge and promoting understanding, supporting reflection, learning and potentially change, game narrative/metaphors, physical immersion and situated play had a key role.

Learning happened as a result of situated play, activating a significant two-level immersion: into the game as a narrative-based system, and into the physical environment wherein players can (more or less) safely make experiences of the topic addressed.

Conclusion

Moving from theory into practice allowed us to clarify some real difficulties that spring from using games as systems for learning about what we consider normal in terms of social interaction. Since the game is not intended for teaching, but rather for sharing perspectives and prompt identification with someone who suffers of social anxiety, understanding whether it was effective requires an in-depth analysis.

In consequence of noticing that the comprehension of the game and its logics largely benefitted from the collective reasoning that took place during the focus groups, further developments would include:

1. extended individual in-depth interviews to better understand the players' subjective interpretation of the game mechanics and metaphors;
2. focus group with people who actually suffer of the disorder portrayed through the game.

The research is still in progress and some limits can be outlined. Firstly it's necessary to improve quantitative data collection able to sharply depict the progressive acquisition of awareness about the topic dealt. Secondly it's fundamental to refine pre- and post- experiences questionnaires in order to measure and highlight potential changes in the mindset of players as well as an increased knowledge about the issues covered. Furthermore the research, to be extended out of the academia and of the design field, needs the involvement of researchers and professionals in psychology and sociology in order to fully understand its potentials.

Guidelines

1. The use of a *stealth approach* (Flanagan and Kaufman, 2015; Kaufman, Flanagan and Seidman, 2016) allowed players to approach the topic with unbiased openness.

2. The inclusion of dynamics that aroused *frustration* and *awkwardness* (Juul, 2013; Mariani, 2016) resulted into source of first-hand comprehension.

3. Support and facilitate forms of collective reasoning between players, since the presence of multiple perspectives nurtures a broader understanding of the game and its elements, as well as of the topic it addresses.

References

Anolli, L., 2011. *La sfida della mente multiculturale. Nuove forme di convivenza.* Milan: Raffaello Cortina.

Antonacci, F., Bertolo, M. and Mariani, I., 2017. In Migrants' Shoes. A Game to Raise Awareness and Support Long-lasting Learning. *Italian Journal of Educational Technology*, [e-journal]. http://dx.doi.org/10.17471/2499-4324/858

Bateson, G., 1956. *The Message "This Is Play".* New York: Josiah Macy Jr. Foundation.

Bogost, I., 2007. *Persuasive Games. The Expressive Power of Videogames.* Cambridge: MIT Press.

Gee J. P., 2003. *What Video Games Have to Teach Us About Learning and Literacy.* New York: Palgrave Macmillan.

Gee J. P., 2004. *Situated Language and Learning: A Critique of Traditional Schooling.* Routledge, New York.

Kaufman, G. and Flanagan, M., 2015. A Psychologically "Embedded" Approach to Designing Games for Prosocial Causes. *Cyberpsychology: Journal of Psychosocial Research on Cyberspace*, 9(3), article 5. http://dx.doi.org/10.5817/CP2015-3-5

Kaufman, G., Flanagan, M. and Seidman, M., 2016. Creating stealth game interventions for attitude and behavior change: An" Embedded Design" model. *Transactions of the Digital Games Research Association*, [e-journal] 2(3). Available at: <http://todigra.org/index.php/todigra/article/view/57> [Accessed 14 May 2017].

Juul, J., 2013. *The Art of Failure: An Essay on the Pain of Playing Video Games.* Cambridge/London: MIT Press.

Mariani, I., 2016. *Meaningful Negative Experiences within Games for Social Change. Designing and Analysing Games as Persuasive Communication Systems.* Ph.D Politecnico di Milano. Available at: <hdl.handle.net/10589/117855> [Accessed 14.05.2017].

Mariani, I., and Gandolfi, E., 2016. Negative Experiences as Learning Trigger: A Play Experience Empirical Research on a Game for Social Change Case Study. *International Journal of Game-Based Learning*, [e-journal] 6(3), pp.50-73. http://dx.doi.org/10.4018/IJGBL.201607010.

Spallazzo, D. and Mariani, I., (in-press). LBMGs and Boundary Objects. Negotiations of Meaning Between Real and Unreal. In *Sociotechnical Environments Conference, STS Proceedings.* Trento, 24-26 November 2017.

McDonald, S., 2005. Studying actions in context: a qualitative shadowing method for organizational research. *Qualitative Research*, [e-journal] 5(4), 455-473. Available at: <http://journals.sagepub.com/doi/pdf/10.1177/1468794105056923> [Accessed 14 May 2017].

Mezirow, J., 1996. Contemporary Paradigms of Learning. *Adult Education Quarterly,* 46(3), 158-172.

Millen, D. R., 2000. Rapid ethnography: time deepening strategies for HCI field research. In: *Proceedings of the 3rd conference on Designing interactive systems: processes, practices, methods, and techniques,* pp. 280-286. http://dx.doi.org/10.1145/347642.347763

Quircio V., 2016. *In ansia. Quando giocare costruisce resilienza.* MSc Politecnico di Milano Ph.D. Available at: <hdl.handle.net/10589/125443> [Accessed 14.05.2017].

Salen, K., 2008. *The Ecology of Games: Connecting Youth, Games, and Learning.* Cambridge: MIT Press.

Schrier K. and Gibson D. eds., 2015. *Ethics and Game Design: Teaching Values Through Play.* Hershey: IGI Global.

Sclavi, M., 2003. *Arte di ascoltare e mondi possibili.* Milan: Pearson.

Schechner, R., 1981. Restoration of Behavior. *Studies in Visual Communication*, 7(3), pp.2-45.

Sicart, M., 2011. Against procedurality. *Game Studies, 11*(3). Available at: <http://gamestudies.org/1103/articles/sicart_ap> [Accessed 14 May 2017].

Sicart, M., 2014). *Play Matters.* Cambridge: MIT Press.

Turner, V., 1982. *From Ritual to Theatre.* New York: Paj Publications.

CONTRIBUTORS

Dr. Jodi Asbell-Clarke, TERC
Jodi Asbell-Clarke has been designing and researching curriculum and professional development for STEM teachers for over 20 years. Jodi's background includes an MA in Math, an MSc in Astrophysics, and a PhD in Education. She was an onboard software verification analyst for IBM during the first 25 missions of the Space Shuttle and taught at the laboratory school at University of Illinois. She has been the principal investigator or numerous curriculum development, teacher professional development, and educational research projects examining the inclusion of all learners in quality STEM education. In 2009, she co-founded EdGE at TERC, a team of game designers, educators, and researchers studying implicit STEM learning in digital games

Ms. Tracey Cassells, Institute of Technology Carlow
Tracey Cassells graduated from IT Carlow with a B.Sc (Hons) in Computer Games Development and is currently enrolled as a Doctorate student. Her research interests are in gamification and the effect of game-elements on time-management.

Karina Dube
Karina Dubé received her BS in Electrical Engineering from the University of Notre Dame, USA, and her MSc in Interactive Media from University College Cork. She is currently working in industry as a front end developer on a statistical analysis web application for process improvement professionals.

Prof. Joseph Eustace, University College Cork
Prof Joseph Eustace: is the Director of the HRB Clinical Research Facility at UCC (CRF-C). The facility Is co-funded by the University and by the Health Research Board and supports the design, conduct and analysis of Patient Focused Research throughout UCC and its affiliated Medical Centres. He is also a Consultant Renal Physician at Cork University Hospital. He graduated MB, BAO BCh (UCD) 1990 and undertook postgraduate training in General Internal Medicine and Nephrology in Dublin (1990-1996), Johns Hopkins University Hospital, Baltimore (1996-1999), and a NIH funded Fellowship in Clinical Epidemiology at the Johns Hopkins Bloomberg School of Public Health, (1997-1999), as part of which he undertook a MHS (Clin Epi) degree. He served as an Assistant Professor on both the Johns Hopkins Faculty of Internal Medicine and in the Department of Clinical Epidemiology and served as State Commissioner for kidney disease, Maryland Kidney Commission (2002 – 2005). He was appointed Consultant (2005) and Professor (2012) in the Department of Nephrology at Cork University Hospital and Director of the CRF-C in 2012. His research has been funded by the NIH (NIDDK), NKF and the HRB and is focused on the nutritional management of CKD and investigations into bone and vascular health in renal transplant recipients.

Dr. Jennifer Killham, University of Cincinnati
Jennifer E. Killham, Ph.D., has devoted over twenty years to fostering intellectual curiosity and divergent thinking through gameful learning. Each day, with zest and enthusiasm, she recommits herself to mentoring emerging talent in the games industry and teaching profession. Jennifer serves on the leadership team for the International Ambassador scholarship program, an organization that promotes diversity in the games industry for underserved regions of the world. In her university-level teaching, Jennifer works with early childcare providers to advance the transformative power of games. Together, alongside these dedicated educators, she reinvigorates learners through the power of play. Jennifer's research combines gameful learning and resilience pedagogy, including the facilitation of an online character play used to develop conflict resolution strategies and the creation of a board game to address affluence and poverty in schooling. She is the author of "Unmasking the Mystique: Utilizing Narrative Character-Playing Games to Support English Language Fluency," which appeared in the International Journal of Game-Based Learning, and the book chapter, "The Power of Feedback: Teachers and Parents Providing Social Motivations in Game-Based Learning" from the book Game-Based Learning and the Power of Play: exploring evidence, challenges and future directions. When not at work, she is often found playing Kyle Brockman's hidden role game Witchhunt or liking pictures of pugs on Instagram.

Dr. Ilaria Mariani, Politecnico di Milano
PhD in Design, Ilaria is research fellow (Design Department) and contract professor (School of Design) at Politecnico di Milano. She designs, investigates and lectures in games for social change as systems for communication and social innovation. Her theoretical and applied research mainly addresses (1) the meaningful negative experiences certain games create to activate reflection and change, and (2) games as empowering interactive narratives, between ethics and aesthetics. The focus is on games able to meaningfully challenge players to explore civic, social, political, moral or ethical issues, encouraging an alteration of entrenched attitudes and sometimes even behaviours. To comprehend the impact on players and their effectiveness in transferring meanings, she employs interdisciplinary practices and tools (quantitative + qualitative). She is part of ImagisLab group (imagislab.it), where she designs and researches games as communication systems and interactive narratives with communitarian interests.

Mr. David Murphy, University College Cork
Mr. David Murphy is a lecturer and researcher at University College Cork; he has a wide range of expertise and experience in the area of Virtual Reality, Spatial Audio and Serious Games.

Ms. Kasyoka Mwanzia, Aalborg University
Kasyoka Mwanzia is from Nairobi, Kenya. She received a B.A., Communication Design, jointly from Concordia University Wisconsin and Milwaukee Institute of Art and Design in 1999. She then worked in various capacities in advertising, marketing and non-profit organisations in Nairobi, and from 2009 to 2015 as a communications consultant. She is currently part of the Media Arts Cultures program – an Erasmus Mundus joint master degree developed by a consortium of four universities. She has studied at the Danube University, Austria; City University, Hong Kong; and Aalborg University, Denmark. Her research interests include global cross border perspectives on: visual and

digital literacy, social contexts of media culture, cross sections between historical and contemporary cultural heritage, cultural mediation, and games for change.

Dr. Daire O'Broin, Institute of Technology Carlow
Daire O Broin holds a Ph.D. in Computer Science from Trinity College Dublin, which focused on approaches to developing the conditions of flow. He has been a lecturer at IT Carlow since 2008, where he teaches on the Computer Games Development programme. His research interests include increasing engagement and intrinsic motivation in games and learning

Prof. Barry Plant, University College Cork
Prof Barry Plant: MB, BCH BAO, BMed SC, MD, FRPCI is a consultant respiratory physician, the Director of the Adult Cystic Fibrosis Centre at Cork University Hospital (CUH)- University College Cork, an executive member of the Cystic Fibrosis Registry of Ireland, the current Chairman of the Medical and Scientific Council of Cystic Fibrosis Ireland, and a former national co-chair for the European Cystic Fibrosis Conference (ECFC). A University College Cork medical graduate, he dual trained in respiratory and general medicine in accordance with the Royal College of Physicians of Ireland and subsequently undertook a fellowship in pulmonary and critical medicine at the University of Washington, Seattle, with a special interest in cystic fibrosis (CF), where he remained until securing his current post in 2007. Prof Plant's research group focuses on translational CF medicine including CF aging, CFTR modulation and the microbiome (lung and gut). Recently he was successfully awarded an FP7 award (6 million Euros over 3 years) from the EU commission, involving 12 partner sites across Europe and one in the USA. The project CFMATTERS (www.cfmatters.eu) will provide a randomised, multi-centre control trial of microbiome-derived antimicrobial treatments versus current empirical therapy and explore the implications of the 'lung-gut' axis with serial prospective lung and gut microbiome analysis in stability and exacerbation in patients with CF. Professor Plant is widely published and recently contributed to both the ERS CF Monograph and the ECFS "Living longer with CF". He has been a Principal Investigator on a wide range of clinical trials and 'real-world' studies in CF. He has been an invited speaker at many scientific meetings including ATS, ERS, Australasian CFC, ECFC, and an FDA meeting.

Ms. Valeria Quircio, Politecnico di Milano
Valeria attended the School of Design, Politecnico di Milano and holds a MSc in Communication Design. She is currently attending the Brand Communication Specializing Master at Politecnico di Milano. She is interested in games as systems of communication, and the relation between them and social issues. In particular, she analysed on how games can become activators of good practices and critical reflections, looking at how they can affect people's behaviors and attitudes. She investigates games as sources of both social engagement and experience-based learning models. During her MSc she created Noar, a persuasive urban game aimed at sensitizing players about the timely but often neglected issue of social anxiety, and that is also intended for triggering thoughtful reflection about our ordinary and extra-ordinary social interactions. Now, she is focusing on how ludic methods and processes can be applied to the Corporate Social Responsibility field, in order to design participative and effective communications.

Dr. Elizabeth Rowe, TERC

Elizabeth Rowe is a senior researcher at TERC, studies and develops innovative uses of technology in and out of schools with a current focus on game-based learning. Dr. Rowe is currently the Director of Researcher for the Educational Gaming Environments group at TERC where she oversees the research design, data collection, and analysis for all EdGE projects. Prior to joining EdGE, she was PI of Kids' Survey Network, co-PI of the Learning Science Online project, and led several formative and summative evaluations of technology integration projects. Elizabeth's background includes a Bachelor's degree in Math from the University of the Pacific and a M.A and Ph.D. in Human Development and Family Studies from Cornell University.

Dr. Sabin Tabirca, University College Cork

Dr Sabin Tabirca: graduated from Faculty of Mathematics of University of Bucharest with a 1H degree in Informatics. He obtained his PhD in 1998 from University of Brunel for studying new sequential and parallel methods for the maximum flow problem. He served as an assistant professor, lecturer, senior lecturer and associate professor in the Computer Science Department of Transylvania University of Brasov for more than 10 years. In 2000, after a short post-doctoral stage in University of Manchester, Dr Tabirca moved to UCC as a lecturer in Computer Science. Since 2010 Dr Tabirca holds a position of senior lecturer.

Mr. You Yuan Tan, University College Cork

You Yuan Tan graduated from University College Cork with a 2H1 degree in Computer Science in 2014. He also completed his Masters with 1H degree in computer Science in University College Cork too. His MSc project was a mobile application for helping Cystic Fibrosis patient.

Ms. Tamara Vagg, University College Cork

Tamara Vagg completed her primary B.A. in Visual Communications in Waterford Institute of Technology in 2012, she went on to complete her Masters in Interactive Media in University College Cork, Tamara's MSc project was proposed by the CFMATTERS research group and specialised in visualisation and simulation for the education of Cystic Fibrosis. Following on from this, she began her PhD in 2014 under the supervision of Dr Sabin Tabirca of UCC and Professor Barry Plant of CUH, and is currently working on developing her MSc research further through this. Tamara has particular interests in patient education design thinking, 3D visuals and simulation. These interests extend to include educational and digital content for other areas of the medical industry

Printed in Great
Britain
by Amazon

32424897R00045